Welcome to this sampler of the Kindergarten components in the Units of Study in Opinion, Information, and Narrative Writing series. The first pages of this sampler provide an overview of the units of study. They describe the instructional pathways each unit follows and how this journey is subdivided into bends, or parts. This overview describes how each bend builds on the learning in the previous bend and sets the stage for the learning in the next bend. Likewise, it describes how each larger unit of study builds on the learning in past units and sets the stage for learning in future units and grades. The tables of contents that follow delineate the steps of the journey and map in detail the learning students will see and experience.

The bulk of this sampler is the first bend from Unit 3, *How-To Books: Writing to Teach Others*. This bend, "Writing How-To Books, Step by Step," launches your students' journey into information writing. This in-depth look allows you to see how learning is progressively built in each unit and how students become immersed in the writing process. In addition to mapping your teaching points, minilessons, conferences, and small-group work, each session also includes Lucy's coaching commentary. In these side-column notes, Lucy is at your side explaining proven strategies, offering professional insight, and coaching you through the nitty-gritty details of teaching.

Also included are samples of the instructional resources that support these core units. *Writing Pathways* shows you the types of learning progressions, checklists, and benchmark writing samples that will help you evaluate your students' work and establish where students are in their writing development. *If… Then… Curriculum* describes the alternate units you can use to enhance or differentiate your instruction. The samples from the resources CD-ROM show you the wealth of teaching tools that support each unit. And finally, the trade book pack lists the mentor texts that support instruction.

As you review this Kindergarten sampler, it is important to remember that the goal of this series is to model thoughtful, reflective teaching in ways that enable you to extrapolate guidelines and methods, so that you will feel ready to invent your own clear, sequenced, vibrant instruction in writing.

> *There is perhaps no year more crucial than kindergarten. What students learn this first year provides the building blocks not just for each subsequent year's instruction and learning, but more importantly, for children's experience of the written word and their identities as people who write. In many cases, it will be you who will introduce kids to the world of written language.*
>
> **—Lucy Calkins**

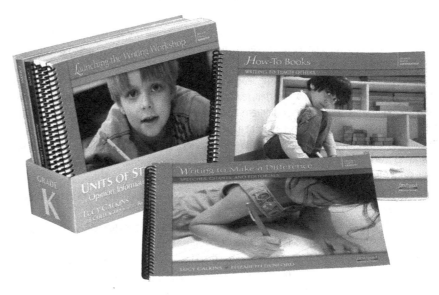

Launching the Writing Workshop

Lucy Calkins and Amanda Hartman

This unit is divided into four sections—four bends in the road. During the first bend you will introduce youngsters to a writing workshop. "You are an author," you'll say, and you'll help youngsters understand how to think up a topic, draw it, and then do their best approximation of writing. Soon, you'll teach children to linger longer and invest more in a piece of writing—thus launching an elementary school career of learning to elaborate! You'll also teach youngsters how to go from finishing one piece to starting another with some independence. In no time, children will use letters as well as pictures to represent meaning. Your youngsters will develop phonemic awareness as they stretch out, listen to, distinguish and record the sounds in a word.

The second bend in the road is titled "Writing Teaching Books." During this portion of the unit, children learn that they can reread what they have written, realize they have more to say, then staple on more pages to make a homemade book. You'll channel children's eagerness to fill up all the pages in their book into a willingness to label more of their pictures, represent more sounds in a word, and make two-word labels.

Things change dramatically in the third bend, "Writing Stories." So far children will have learned that they can write to teach others all about whatever they know. Now they learn that they can also write to capture true stories from their lives. They will draw what happened first, then touch the page and tell the story, then write the story of that one time. Your children will be eager to learn the tricks of the trade, so you'll teach some early lessons in narrative craft.

In the last bend your children will select a few stories to publish and will learn to revise and edit as they make those stories the best they can be. To do this, you'll introduce children to the writing checklists that will undergird every unit of study. With guidance from the checklists and from you, children will make their best writing better. They'll add detail, fix spelling, and get more sounds into their words. Then, to culminate the unit, students will celebrate by reading selections from their writing to a circle of classmates.

Welcome to Unit 1

BEND I ✦ We Are All Writers

1. **We Are All Writers: Putting Ideas on Paper with Pictures and Words**

   In this session, you'll teach students that young writers think of something that they know about and use pictures and words to put their ideas on paper.

2. **Writers Know that "When We Are Done, We Have Just Begun."**

   In this session, you'll teach students that writers look back at their writing and see if they can add more to it.

3. **Carrying on Independently as Writers**

   In this session, you'll teach students that writers come up with solutions to their problems and carry on writing.

4. **Writers Call to Mind What They Want to Say, Then Put That onto the Page**

   In this session, you'll teach students that writers picture what they want to write about first and then put all of the details onto the page.

5. **Stretching Out Words to Write Them**

   In this session, you'll teach students that young writers say words slowly and then write down the sounds that they hear.

6. **Writing Even Hard-To-Write Ideas**

   In this session, you'll teach students that when writers have an idea that is hard to draw or a word that is hard to spell, they don't quit. Writers keep trying.

CONTENTS

Writing for Readers

Lucy Calkins and Natalie Louis

Until now you've so wanted your children to feel good as writers that you have hidden your struggles to translate their spindly letters into meaning. When neither you nor the child could decipher a text, you have turned quickly to the picture or to the next story. The problem is that the only reason children will care about spelling, punctuation, or white space is that these conventions make it easier for others to read and to appreciate their texts! It's crucial, therefore, that as soon as children have the ability to begin to write in ways a reader could conceivably read, you let them in on the truth. This unit of study begins with you, as a teacher, confessing to your children that you have a hard time reading their writing. You'll quickly follow with an invitation to children to review their stories as readers, making a pile of the ones that are clear and another pile of the ones that still need work. As you review the piles, you will discover ways to tailor the lessons in this first bend to meet the individual needs of your students. Early in this bend, you'll encourage children to draw on all they know about writing stories. As children work, you will encourage them to write words in more conventional ways, use drawing to plan, write in sentences, and reread their work as they write.

In Bend II you'll give your students additional tools and opportunities to make their writing more powerful and clearer for their readers. You'll begin by teaching children how to use a checklist to reflect on what they have learned so far this year. The next two lessons are designed to strengthen your students' word-writing skills by spotlighting the use of vowels and sight words. To balance this close-in focus, you'll next teach children to listen for and capture their true storytelling words, not just the easy-to-spell words. In the next few lessons you will teach your writers the power of partnerships as they aim to make their writing clearer, using everything they have learned to make writing that is easy for readers to read.

In Bend III the focus shifts from getting readable words on the page to telling stories more powerfully through revision. In the first lesson, you'll teach your writers how to mine their drawings to find more stories to tell. The middle lessons of this bend teach your children how to use flaps to make additions to stories. In the final lesson children work as partners to help each other make their stories clearer and easier to read.

In the final bend you'll challenge your kids to use all they have learned about revision and editing to make one of their pieces shine. Children will work on creating more satisfying endings and on making their pieces beautiful and ready for a larger audience. This is also an opportunity for writers to assess the work they have done. The final celebration of this unit might be making a bulletin board or reading work out loud to an audience.

Welcome to Unit 2

BEND I ✦ Writing Stories That People Can Really *Read*

1. **Writing for Readers**

   In this session, you'll teach students that writers reread their writing to make sure that it is easy to read. If it is not, they go back and fix it up so that others can read it.

2. **How to Write True Stories that Readers Really Want to Read**

   In this session, you'll teach students that writers call upon what they have already learned. Specifically, you'll teach them how to go back to old anchor charts on narrative writing and use them in their new writing.

3. **Drawing Stories for Readers**

   In this session, you'll elaborate on the process children use when they go about writing every day. You will teach children how to draw and talk about what they need in order to tell their story.

4. **Writing Sentences That Tell a Story**

   In this session, you'll teach students that writers write sentences. You'll help them transition their stories from drawings to sentences that tell their true story.

5. **The Power of Rereading**

   In this session, you'll teach students that for a variety of reasons, writers reread often. They write a little and then read a little, flipping back and forth between being a writer and a reader.

How-To Books
Writing to Teach Others

Lucy Calkins, Laurie Pessah, and Elizabeth Moore

There are four bends in the road in this unit. Although the instructional focus changes a bit as your children progress through the unit, you will continue to expect them to write lots and lots of how-to texts. At the start, you'll tell children that writers not only use writing to tell stories, they also use writing to teach others how to do things, and you'll show them a how-to text. They'll have no trouble seeing that writers of how-to texts teach the steps for doing something, and they'll probably also notice that the steps are numbered and there are drawings for each step. You will then surprise kids by saying, "So, right now, go and write your very own how-to book!"

Because children will be writing what they know how to do, they'll bring their areas of expertise into your classroom. You will discover the hidden talents of your young writers as they write books on everything from How to Make an Ice Cream Sundae to How to Change a Diaper," to "How to Hit A Home Run," to "How to Do Yoga. There will be lessons on drawing and writing one step at a time and writing with enough clarity and detail that others can follow the directions. Writing partners will play an important role in this bend, as pairs of children test their directions to make sure everything makes sense and get ideas from each other.

Lessons in the second bend focus on studying mentor texts and trying out techniques the students notice in those texts, including tucking tips into their teaching and using the "you" voice to write directly to readers. Many How-To texts use comparisons to make their points clear, and you will highlight that as well. Ultimately, you'll want to use this bend to help your young writers understand that they can always look to real, published books as exemplars and then use what they learn.

In Bend III you will help your children find opportunities throughout the school day to write How-To books that can be helpful to others. You'll encourage children to write a series or collection of How-To books for their classmates, so this bend emphasizes writing easy-to-read books that convey to readers exactly what they need to know.

In Bend IV, "Giving How-To Books as Gifts," you will help your children get ready to share their work with its intended audiences. You will teach writers to think strategically about where in the world their books should go: "How To Give a Dog a Bath" might be suited for the neighborhood pet store, while "How To Make Guacamole" might be important for a family member about to hold a party.

Welcome to Unit 3

BEND I ✦ Writing How-To Books, Step by Step

1. **Writers Study the Kind of Writing They Plan to Make**

   In this session, you'll teach students that before a writer writes, he thinks "What kind of thing am I making?" and then studies examples of whatever it is he wants to make.

2. **Writers Use What They Already Know: Touching and Telling the Steps across the Pages**

   In this session, you'll teach students to draw on what they already know about planning, touching, and telling the steps of their how-to books across pages.

3. **Writers Become Readers, Asking, "Can I Follow This?"**

   In this session, you'll teach students that writers reread their writing as they go, making changes along the way.

4. **Writers Answer a Partner's Questions**

   In this session, you'll teach students that writing partners help each other make how-to books clearer and easier to follow.

5. **Writers Label Their Diagrams to Teach Even More Information**

   In this session, you'll teach students that writers add detailed information to their writing by labeling their diagrams.

6. **Writers Write as Many Books as They Can**

   In this session, you could teach students that writers develop the habit of writing faster, longer, and stronger. One way they do this is by setting goals for themselves.

7. **Writers Reflect and Set Goals to Create Their Best Information Writing**

   In this session, you'll teach students that writers draw on all they have learned about information writing, and they use an information writing checklist to set writing goals.

CONTENTS

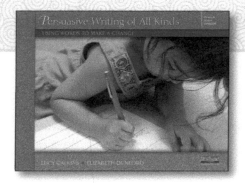

Persuasive Writing of All Kinds
Using Words to Make a Change

Lucy Calkins and Elizabeth Dunford

In this unit children do lots of lots of persuasive writing. They begin by writing signs, songs, petitions, and letters about problems they see in their classroom, then in their school, then in the larger world of their neighborhood. The first portion of the unit—the first bend in the road—is "Exploring Opinion Writing: Making Our School a Better Place." From the very start of this unit, you'll ask children to look at the world, seeing not just what is but what could be. You'll teach children to reflect on problems, think about what could make things better, and then write to help make a change. This is not a time to assign students a particular genre or particular issue; instead you will offer a menu and urge them to consider even more ways they could write to make a change: a book, a song, a card, a letter—the choices are endless.

Regardless of the genre, your kindergartners will be learning to make words (and pictures) to express what they want to happen and convince an audience that it should. You'll help students publish their work by posting signs in the hallways, reading pieces to schoolmates in other classrooms, reciting songs over the school loudspeaker, and using a bullhorn to rally friends to sign a petition during recess. As children send their words out into the school, they'll learn that by writing they can convince others to make the world better.

In the second bend you'll channel students to write lots of persuasive letters. You'll teach writers that in order to make a change in the world, it helps to ask, "Who could help me fix this problem?" and then write letters to persuade people to join the cause. You'll help children write lots of these letters, to lots of people, addressing lots of problems. You'll teach children that including facts and information in this kind of letter helps make it more persuasive, and you'll again give students an opportunity to publish their work, perhaps with a class trip to the post office or to the nearest mailbox.

In the final bend you'll rally kids to join you in a whole-class pursuit around a more global cause, perhaps protecting the planet. You'll again invite children to write in a variety of genres, working on individual projects that convince others to "be green!" You'll remind writers to recall everything they have learned about persuasive writing this month and apply these strategies when writing new pieces, and you'll also teach them ways to lift the level of their persuasive writing.

To prepare for the final publication, you'll provide opportunities for partners to plan how their presentations might go, how they might use body language to show the big messages they have about their topic. You'll help your young politicians learn ways writers captivate their audience. You'll celebrate and publish the persuasive writing your students have worked on during the unit, reminding them of the larger purpose—sharing opinions and convincing others to make a change.

Welcome to Unit 4

BEND I ✦ Exploring Opinion Writing: Making Our School a Better Place

1. **Words Are Like Magic Wands: They Can Make Things Happen**

   In this session, you'll teach students that just as magicians use magic wands to make things happen, writers use words.

2. **Convincing People: Providing Reasons and Consequences**

   In this session, you'll teach students that the more reasons they can provide, the more convincing their writing will be.

3. **Don't Stop There! Generating More Writing for More Causes**

   In this session, you'll teach students that opinion writers cast a wide net when writing, writing in a variety of genres and to a variety of audiences.

4. **Writers Reread and Fix Up Their Writing**

   In this session, you'll teach students that writers do not wait for others to tell them how to revise their writing. They reread what they have written and think, "What can I do to make my writing better?"

5. **Spelling Strategies Give Writers Word Power**

   In this session, you'll teach students that writers call upon many strategies to figure out how to write words that are hard to spell.

6. **Hear Ye! Hear Ye! Writing to Spread the Word (a Mini-Celebration)**

   In this session, you'll teach students that opinion writers get their words out into the world to enable change.

CONTENTS

CONTENTS

If... Then... Curriculum
Assessment-Based Instruction

Lucy Calkins *with Colleagues from the Teachers College Reading and Writing Project*

Introduction: Kindergarten Writers and Planning Your Year

Part One: Alternate and Additional Units

Storytelling across the Pages: First Steps for Personal Narrative Writing

IF your students are still not writing simple sequenced narratives by the end of the Launching the Writing Workshop *unit OR your students are writing letters or words on the page without any meaning or story to go with them, THEN you might want to teach this unit before* Writing for Readers.

Looking Closely: Observing, Labeling, and Listing Like Scientists

IF, after teaching the Launching the Writing Workshop *unit, you feel that your students could use some additional practice with labeling and writing simple sentences, THEN you might want to teach this unit. If your science curriculum is not underway at this early point in the year, however, you may want to delay this unit until that curricular area is up and running.*

Writing Pattern Books to Read, Write, and Teach

IF your students are starting to read beginning reader leveled pattern books and you want to immerse them in a writing unit that goes hand in hand with their reading, THEN you might want to teach this unit.

Writing All-About Books

IF you want to give your students an opportunity to write expository informational texts about their own areas of personal expertise, THEN you may want to teach this unit. It builds on the work of How-To Books: Writing to Teach Others.

Music in Our Hearts: Writing Songs and Poetry

IF you want to teach your students to become more conscious of the crafting and language decisions that writers make, THEN you might want to teach this unit.

With a Little Help from My Friends: Independent Writing Projects across the Genres

IF you want to present your students with an opportunity to make independent decisions about which genres to express their ideas in, as well as provide them with the chance to reflect on their growth as writers throughout their kindergarten year, THEN you might want to end the school year with this unit.

Part Two: Differentiating Instruction for Individuals and Small Groups: If... Then... Conferring Scenarios

NARRATIVE WRITING

Structure and Cohesion

If the writer is new to this particular genre . . .
If the story is confusing or seems to be missing important information . . .
If there are multiple stories in the booklet . . .
If the story lacks focus . . .

Elaboration

If the writer has created a story that is sparse in pictures and words . . .
If the writer spends more time adding insignificant details to the picture, rather than elaborating with words onto the story . . .
If the writer tells action, action, action and seems not to elaborate on any of the options . . .
If the writer overuses one kind of detail more than others to elaborate . . .

Language

If the writer has few if any words on the page . . .
If the writer has words on the page, but they are difficult to read . . .

The Process of Generating Ideas

If the writer struggles with thinking about an idea for a story . . .
If the writer returns to the same story repeatedly . . .

The Process of Drafting

If the writer starts many new pieces but just gives up on them halfway through. . .
If the writer tends to write short pieces with few words or sentences . . .
If the writer's folder lacks volume of pieces . . .

The Process of Revision

If the writer rarely adds to the writing without prompting and support . . .
If the writer usually adds to his writing rather than taking things away . . .
If the writer tends to revise by elaborating, rather than narrowing and finding the focus of the piece . . .

The Process of Editing

If the writer does not use what he knows to edit his piece . . .
If the writer does not know what in her piece needs editing . . .

INFORMATION WRITING

Structure and Cohesion

If the writer is new to this particular genre . . .
If the writer has included facts as he thinks about them . . .

Elaboration

If the writer provides information in vague or broad ways . . .
If the writer writes with lots of good information but it is in helter-skelter order . . .
If the writer invents or makes up information about the topic in order to elaborate . . .

Language

If the writer does not use all that he knows about letter sounds/vowel patterns to write words . . .
If the writer does not use domain-specific vocabulary . . .

The Process of Generating Ideas

If the writer chooses ideas that she likes rather than what she actually knows information about . . .

The Process of Drafting

If the writer spends more time elaborating on his drawing than using the picture to help add and write more information . . .

The Process of Revision

If the writer is unsure how to revise her writing and does not use the various tools in the classroom . . .

If the writer tends to revise by elaborating, rather than narrowing and finding the focus of the text or chapter . . .

The Process of Editing

If the writer edits quickly and feels done, missing many errors . . .

OPINION WRITING

Structure and Cohesion

If the writer is new to the writing workshop or this particular genre of writing . . .

Elaboration

If the writer is struggling to elaborate . . .
If the writer uses some elaboration strategies some of the time . . .
If the writer's piece lacks voice . . .

Language

If the writer struggles to write longer or "harder" words on the page . . .
If the writer tends to not use specific and precise language as she writes about her opinions . . .

The Process of Generating Ideas

If the writer is stymied to come up with an idea for writing . . .
If the writer writes one piece, then another, without making any one her best . . .

The Process of Drafting

If the writer doesn't have a plan before he begins to write . . .

The Process of Revision

If the writer fills the pages as she drafts and only writes to the bottom of the page when she revises . . .

If the writer tends to have a limited repertoire of how to elaborate on his topic . . .

The Process of Editing

If the writer edits for one thing but not for others . . .
If the writer only uses or knows one way to edit her spelling . . .

SAMPLE BEND

Writers Study the Kind of Writing They Plan to Make

IN THIS SESSION, you'll teach students that before a writer writes, he thinks "What kind of thing am I making?" and then studies examples of whatever it is he wants to make.

GETTING READY

✔ Ribbon and scissors, for a ribbon-cutting ceremony (with an upbeat musical selection in the background) (see Connection)

✔ Pictures of a variety of dogs large enough to be seen by children when sitting in the meeting area (see Teaching) ⊗

✔ Previously created "true story" (make multiple copies, enough for one per table) and "How to Draw" class texts from the *Writing for Readers* unit (see Teaching and Active Engagement)

✔ A simple narrative (see Active Engagement)

✔ A child's how-to book from your collection from past years, from a student from another class, or your own child-version how-to book (see Active Engagement)

✔ Basket of how-to books, one basket for each table. The basket can be labeled "How-To Books" and can include published texts as well as children's writing.

✔ Two types of prestapled how-to booklets for children to choose from on a tray at each table. You may want to offer booklets of three pages and five pages, with 3–4 or 6–7 lines for writing, along with extra pages that children can add on (see Link). ⊗

✔ A familiar how-to text that you have read with your class several times before beginning this unit of study and a copy of a page from it. This session uses an excerpt from *My First Soccer Game* by Alyssa Satin Capucilli (see Share).

✔ "How-To Writing" chart that you will create during the share.

✔ Chart paper and markers

COMMON CORE STATE STANDARDS: W.K.2, W.K.5, W.K.8, RI.K.1, RI.K.6, RI.K.9, RI.1.6, RI.1.9, SL.K.1, SL.K.2, SL.K.3, L.K.1, L.K.2

D O YOU REMEMBER HOW EXCITING IT WAS, when you were little, to start a new school year? I loved the new school supplies—the pencil case, the erasers that always smelled so good, even that transparent green protractor that never seemed to have a purpose. I remember flipping through the pages of the clean new notebooks ready to be written upon. For me, the start of the year was always a time for new resolutions, for a new identity. "This year," I'd tell myself, *"This year,* I'll record all my assignments in my assignment pad. I'll write in cursive. I'll write a page a day." Underneath any particular resolve was the fervent hope that I could draw a line in the sand and start on a new and better chapter.

The new unit that starts today can become an especially big deal for your children—a whole new chapter in their writing lives—because they will be making a different kind of writing from anything they have ever made before. Whereas during the first two units they wrote stories, they now turn a new leaf and embark on how-to writing. You can also call it *procedural writing* or *functional writing* or *explanatory writing*. The Common Core State Standards cluster this kind of writing under the larger category of informational writing. These standards suggest that one third of children's time across all subjects and across the entire year be devoted to informational writing. So the work that children embark on today will be important. Eventually they will transfer their skills at how-to writing into math, as they detail how they solve a problem, and to science, as they write lab reports that are a variation of this kind of writing.

This session creates a drumroll, then, around the fact that this is new work. Children are taught that when writers approach a piece of writing, they need to think, "What kind of writing is this?" and "How does this kind of writing go?" The fact that a writer pauses to establish the genre in which he is writing may seem obvious to you, but it is not obvious to children. Think, for example, of the fact that children will soon write all-about books, also called *information books,* which will present its own sorts of demands. By the time children are in first grade, all-about books contain different kinds of writing, with a dog book perhaps containing one chapter on kinds of dogs, one on the day I got my dog, and one a how-to text such as "How to Give Your Dog a Bath." If a child pauses at the start of each chapter to ask, "What kind of text am I making?" and realizes that "The Day I Got My Dog" is a narrative and that "How to Give Your Dog a Bath" is a how-to text, each following different conventions, that will be an important feat! That work is still a stretch for most of your students, but it is helpful to teach with an awareness of what lies beyond the immediate future.

"The fact that a writer pauses to establish the genre in which he is writing may seem obvious to you, but it is not obvious to children."

You will see that this session makes no attempt to teach the characteristics of how-to writing in any explicit way. Instead, children are taught that writers study the kind of text they intend to make, noting whatever they can about that text, and then write accordingly. You leave it up to children to inquire into the characteristics of the genre and to discern that this writing is written in tiny numbered steps, that each step is accompanied by a drawing that serves to teach, and so forth. Some of your children will glean these conventions from their review of finished how-to texts; others may not (in which case you can eventually teach this more explicitly). Either way, they will thrive in your confidence and learn from your implicit message that it is a pleasure to work hard, with independence, on a big job—and that writing contains lots of those big jobs.

SESSION 1: WRITERS STUDY THE KIND OF WRITING THEY PLAN TO MAKE

3

Writers Study the Kind of Writing They Plan to Make

CONNECTION

Create a ribbon-cutting ceremony, complete with a song and a proclamation, producing a drumroll around the transition to this new kind of writing.

When the children arrived in the class, they noticed a big red plastic ribbon, preventing anyone from coming to the meeting area. I said nothing about this.

While children were still in their seats, I said, "Writers, this morning I need to tell you that whenever people have built a new bridge or a new library or a new sports stadium, the people organize a ribbon-cutting ceremony for opening day. Before anyone enters the new bridge or library or sports stadium, all the people gather for a ribbon-cutting ceremony. Today we start not only a new unit of study—which is a big deal—but also we start writing a whole new kind of writing! So will all of you gather at the edge of our meeting area for our ceremony?"

Once the children were standing alongside the ribbon, I suggested we sing a writing song—a variation of "If You're Happy and You Know It, Clap Your Hands." I suggested that for our first verse, we sing, "If you're a writer and you know it, clap your hands." Then "If you're a speller," and finally, "If you're a storyteller." Once the song was completed, I took hold of the largest shears I could find, and in a mayoral, commanding voice proclaimed, "Today marks the start of a new unit. As of today, our class will begin a whole new kind of writing." Then we snipped the ribbon, and I announced, "Let the new work begin!" and children thronged to their places.

Name the teaching point.

"Writers, today I want to teach you that just like there are different kinds of dogs, there are different kinds of writing. Before a writer writes, the writer thinks, 'What kind of thing am I making?'"

◆ COACHING

You may alter partnerships for this unit, in which case you'll need a system for conveying the new alliances to children. Partner talkative kids with quieter kids, kids who ask good questions with kids who tend to be vague, English language learners with language models. In some cases you might find triads work well, putting two children who can carry on proficiently together with a third child who can benefit from the modeling.

4

GRADE K: HOW-TO BOOKS

16   *Sample pages from Kindergarten, Unit 3, How-To Books: Writing to Teach Others* — Bend I: "Writing How-To Books, Step by Step"

TEACHING

Point out that there are different kinds of writing, illustrating this with enlarged versions of a familiar narrative and how-to text, suggesting children ascertain the differences.

"What are these?" I asked, holding up pictures of dramatically different dogs. The kids agreed they were dogs, and some called out the specific breeds. I nodded. "You are right. These are all dogs, but they look really different, don't they? That's because they are different kinds of dogs.

"Let me show you something else." I revealed the familiar class story about the bee that came into our class from the previous *Writing for Readers* unit of study that the class had helped to write and, alongside it, the directions we used earlier in the year for how writers draw. "These are both pieces of writing, but they are different kinds of writing. One is a true story of one small moment, and one is how-to writing, or you could call it *directions*. Starting today, we're going to be making how-to books." I gestured to the paper showing directions.

"Before writing, the writer thinks, 'What kind of thing am I making?' and then studies examples of whatever he or she wants to make to learn how to do this new kind of writing.

"Today I thought maybe, just maybe, you could do that work all on your own. Do you think that if I read this how-to writing to you and afterward I zip up my mouth and say *nothing*, you could turn your brain on really, really high and see if *you* can study this new kind of writing and figure out how it goes, how it is different from a story, and then do some of this writing all by yourself?"

The children were game. "This means I am not going to tell you anything about how this new kind of writing goes. I'm just going to read you some examples. I know you can do this. I'll read, and then you'll go to your writing place and make your own how-to book, all by yourself.

They agreed.

Encourage students to choose a topic—something they will teach others to do—before channeling children to study the differences between narratives and how-to texts and to get started writing the latter.

"Before you study how this kind of writing goes, you probably want to have a topic in mind that you will write about today. So think of something you know how to do that you could teach others. Like do you know how to braid hair, or to ride a scooter, or to give a dog a bath, or to make pancakes, or to make a goal?" I left a tiny pool of silence. "You have something in your mind? Thumbs up if you have thought of something you know how to do.

"Okay. What are you planning to teach people to do?" I asked and called on just a few children. "Are you ready to study how this kind of writing goes?"

As children become more experienced writers, they may come to know narrative writing as simply "small moments," due to the emphasis over time on writing focused, detailed narratives. Depending on how your last unit unfolded, it may or may not make sense to begin referring to small moments now. In any case you will want to remind students what they already know about narrative writing.

By rattling off examples of very common, everyday things that students are experts at, we are modeling the kinds of topic choices that are available. Students don't have to dig deep to find interesting topics; the things they do every day are enough.

SESSION 1: WRITERS STUDY THE KIND OF WRITING THEY PLAN TO MAKE   **5**

ACTIVE ENGAGEMENT

Abstaining from citing differences, read a narrative and then two different how-to books. Channel children to discuss what they notice.

I read part of a quick narrative and then shifted to read the "How to Draw" chart (children were familiar with this from *Writing for Readers*), touching the numbers alongside the steps and the informative pictures in a significant ("notice this") fashion.

Then, signaling "Wait," I brought out the work a child had done and read his writing.

LINK

Reiterate that writers think, "What kind of thing am I making?" and encourage children to help each other study what goes into a how-to book and then write one as best they can.

My lips still sealed, I gestured for the children to get going. On each table, there was an example of how-to writing and some blank books. Once the children were at their tables, I said, "You can help each other figure out how this new kind of writing goes and get going writing your own."

You can use the "How to Draw" class text from Writing for Readers, *or you may decide to choose any how-to text that you have written previously. With your class, try to choose a text where the directions have been written with one step on each page, with detailed diagrams or pictures that teach and other features of how-to writing.*

FIG. 1–1   Stapling paper like this into three-page or five-page booklets gives children quick access to the materials they need. You can observe your students at work to determine how many lines per page and how many pages per booklet to offer. Remember to teach kids to select paper that will leave an extra line or two left over, room to add more later.

6

GRADE K: HOW-TO BOOKS

18   Sample pages from Kindergarten, Unit 3, *How-To Books: Writing to Teach Others* — Bend I: "Writing How-To Books, Step by Step"

Welcoming Approximations, Inviting Children into the New Work

TODAY'S CONFERRING AND SMALL-GROUP WORK will be a special pleasure because your main goal will be to rally kids' energy for the exciting new work of this unit. Give yourself a talking-to before you head out around the room. Repeat over and over to yourself, "I will not fuss over whether their work is perfect. I will celebrate approximation. I will celebrate approximation." Plan on enjoying all their mess-ups, for now. If they totally don't get how to write how-to texts, that is absolutely fine. That's why you will be teaching this unit! Imagine how impressive it will be later when you contrast their start of the unit work—today's writing and their on-demand pieces—with their end of the unit work.

So plan to travel quickly among the writers, using table compliments to sprinkle good will and confidence and excitement among them. Pull up to one table where some kids are working. You may note that a few seem oblivious to the fact that this is a new genre, with different conventions. Their writing will look exactly like it looked a week ago. Let that go, for now. Meanwhile, notice that one child is looking at—even just glancing at—the finished how-to book that you left on the table. "Oh my goodness. You all are making such wise decisions—the way you keep on studying the example and keep on noticing the ways that a how-to book is so, so different than storybooks! I am thinking and hoping that if I go to another table and then come back to this one, by then maybe some of you will be talking together while pointing to specific things you notice in your how-to book. Maybe then you can see if any one of you has already done some of the same things that you notice in your own how-to writing! I love the way you know that writers study examples of the kind of writing they want to write and then make their writing the same!"

You may want to carry some Post-its®, or better yet, Post-it flags, with you so that you can encourage children to study and notice features of published how-to texts. It will probably take some doing for you to channel children to notice things such as the format and conventions of the writing, rather than the specific content and information. The child might notice that the author of the washing your dog how-to text does

MID-WORKSHOP TEACHING
Help Children Carry On with Independence

"Writers, can I stop you for a moment?" I waited until their eyes were on me. "I just want to remind you that as soon as you finish one how-to book, you can reread it to make sure it makes sense and then start another one! Don't wait! I see a few of you sitting, waiting. I think you are ready to start a new how-to book! Do it! Get another how-to booklet! You are on a roll. Don't stop now! Go get some paper. You know what to do!"

As Students Continue Working . . .

"In a few minutes we're going to be all out of time. Can you believe it? When I know that my writing time is almost over, I always like to do one last check to make sure that my writing makes sense, sounds right, and looks right. Right now, everybody, reread one page of your writing and ask yourself, 'Does that make sense?'" Then, noticing some writers had yet to start rereading, I said, firmly, "That's right, everybody, right now."

As children worked, I noticed that some of them were rereading their writing, but they had already put away their pens. I said, "Don't forget, you can keep your pen in your hand while you reread so you can revise your writing if you need to. Don't forget, you can use one end of the pen to read and the other end of the pen for writing!"

"Don't forget to point under each word. Check the pictures you drew. Make sure the words match what is in the pictures. If it doesn't match, change it!"

SAMPLE BEND

the job indoors and may wonder why she doesn't use a hose out of doors, and that sort of observation won't exactly help the youngster as she writes her how-to book on braiding hair. You may or may not address this disconnect today. There will be other ways to get at this. For children who have no trouble noticing that how-to writing uses different forms and conventions, you may want to point out that noticing what the author has done is one thing; noticing *how* and speculating *why* are even more challenging and important kinds of intellectual work.

Of course, it is one thing for you to allow kids to approximate within this genre and another for you to allow kids to sit frozen over their paper. You are not apt to find that many children struggle over topic choice, but if a few do, you will need to help them get started. One way to do this is to gather those students around the class "Flow of the Day" chart, telling them that this chart, this daily schedule, can always be a secret source of topics they could teach others. Point to the first thing on the chart. If it says, for example, "Morning Meeting," you can say to children, "I bet you could each write a 'How to Have a Morning Meeting' book, couldn't you? Think, 'What is the first step to having a morning meeting?'" After recalling a few steps that could be included in a book about the first item in the "Flow of the Day" chart, you could progress to the second item on the chart, doing the same work with it. "You could each write a 'How to Have Reading Workshop' book, right? What would be the first step in a reading workshop?"

If you were doing this work with a small group of children, you could then say, "Right now, pick one part of our schedule and give me a thumbs up when you've picked one. Excellent. Now turn to the person next to you and take turns telling your first step. 'Step 1 . . .'" As kids begin to name the steps for the event they chose, coach into this work. After they have named the second step, they should probably get started sketching and writing.

As you can imagine, it helps to carry ideas like that one in your mental pocket, so that when you observe children and decide on ways to teach them, you don't need to invent all your teaching on the spot but can draw on a repertoire of ideas for conferences and small groups. For this reason, it helps to talk with colleagues about some of the things they find themselves teaching kids during the actual workshop. If you and your colleagues share and collect ideas for conferences and small groups that will be especially helpful now, at the start of this unit, notice that those ideas will often be transferable to other units as well. For example, at the start of this unit and every unit, you can powerfully use conferences and small-group time to remind children to bring all they know from previous units into this unit. That is incredibly important instruction that has the potential to make a huge difference. (Think, for example, about whether or not, today, kids are touching and telling, using the word wall, rereading often, and so on, and think how helpful all of that skill work will be to this unit.)

Step 1: Open your drawer. And get your underwear.

Step 2: Open your drawer and get your shirt.

Step 3: Open your drawer and get your jeans.

Step 4: Open the top drawer again and get your socks.

Step 5: Get dressed!

FIG. 1–2   On the first day of the unit, many students will be excited to choose topics they know well from their own experience, and will write an entire booklet in one sitting, like this student did on "How to Get Dressed." Then, in subsequent days, they can go back and add more to each page.

8

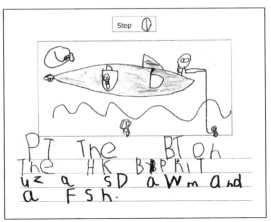

Step 1: *Put the bait on the hook by pinching it. Use a sardine, a worm, and a fish.*

Step 2: *Next cast the line.*

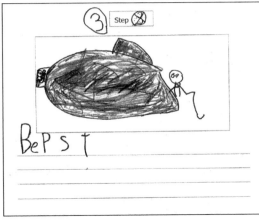

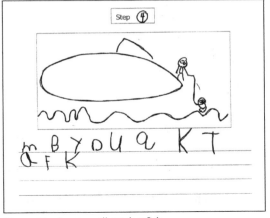

Step 3: *Be patient.*

Step 4: *Maybe you will catch a fish.*

FIG. 1–3   Encourage children to listen for whatever sounds they can hear in a word and to use their alphabet charts and other resources around the room to write words as best they can. There may be students recording mostly initial and ending consonants (like this student, who wrote "How to Go Fishing") right alongside students who spell mostly conventionally.

Compare How-To Writing with Familiar True Stories and Notice Differences

Collect and list a few especially important differences between narrative and how-to writing.

After convening children in the meeting area, I said, "Will someone tell me a way that how-to writing is different than story writing?" I taped a photocopied page from a familiar how-to book, *My First Soccer Game*, to a piece of chart paper, turning the easel so that children could see it from their writing spots where they were still seated. As a few children offered up something about how-to writing, I drew an arrow to the photocopied how-to text to highlight the feature they mentioned. "How-to books have numbers!" exclaimed one student. Using a big marker, I wrote, "Numbers the steps" off to the side of the copied page and drew an arrow pointing to one of the numbered steps. Soon we'd made this chart, with arrows pointing to the parts of the page the children referred to.

How-To Writing

1. Tells what to do, in steps.

2. Numbers the steps.

3. Has a picture for each step.

"As we learn more about how-to writing, we will talk more about how writers go about making books like this to teach people how to do many things."

How-To Writing

✓ 1. Tells what to do, in steps.

✓ 2. Numbers the steps.

✓ 3. Has a picture for each step.

Charts are more memorable and meaningful for kids when you create them together. Often you can simply write the chart along with kids. In this case, the chart was prepared ahead of time, minus the checkmarks on Post-its. Then the Post-its were added as the children discussed each item. Notice that the chart leaves room to add more.

10

GRADE K: HOW-TO BOOKS

22

Sample pages from Kindergarten, Unit 3, How-To Books: Writing to Teach Others — Bend I: "Writing How-To Books, Step by Step"

Writers Use What They Already Know

Touching and Telling the Steps across the Pages

Y ESTERDAY YOUR EMPHASIS was on the fact that writers think, "What kind of thing am I making?" and realize that just as there are different kinds of dogs, there are also different kinds of writing. You invited youngsters to look hard at a piece of writing, thinking, "How does this piece of writing go?" and you channeled them to study examples of how-to writing to identify features of the new genre. Some of them will have done this successfully, and some will need your help. Today you provide that help in a way that suggests you are merely compiling all that they noticed from their careful study.

As you do this, remember the advice from Stephen Covey: first things first. Your goal is not to deluge children with an overwhelmingly large inventory of every conceivable trait of procedural writing. So this means you will not want to ask repeatedly, "What else do you notice that authors of how-to writing do? What else? What else?" For example, writers of how-to books often include little warnings or cautionary notes. There is no reason to mention this now, and in fact doing so takes the wind out of a later minilesson.

You can collect answers from children while still shaping the eventual list by asking children to turn and talk about their observations, eavesdropping, and then calling on children whose observations are especially foundational. You can also add more observations to the list you collect. "Did some of you also notice that . . . ?" you can say, and then articulate whatever you wish your children had contributed.

As you talk about the characteristics of how-to writing, you'll weave in examples of this writing, helping to prime the pump so that children generate topics they will write about today. Some children may not have finished yesterday's how-to book and may need to return to it, but in general, your expectation can be that children will write at least one of these books each day. Whereas many will start the unit off by writing a few words for each step in the process, before long you'll be expecting closer to two or three sentences for each step.

IN THIS SESSION, you'll teach students that writers draw on what they already know about planning, touching, and telling the steps of their how-to books across pages.

GETTING READY

✔ Booklets (with extra pages that children can add on) in a tray on each table. On each page, there will be a box for children to number the steps.

✔ Children will come to the meeting area with their writing folders today (see Connection).

✔ "How-To Writing" anchor chart, created in Session 1 (see Connection and Share)

✔ How-to writing piece from a student, either one that you have saved from a previous year or from a student in another class or Cooper Loval's piece on the CD (see Connection and Share)

✔ Students' writing from the previous session (see Connection)

✔ Enlarged version of the booklets the children are using for shared writing. You can prepare half sheets of chart paper with a box for sketching and lines for writing to look just like the paper the children use (see Teaching).

✔ Idea for a class how-to book that you and the children will begin making during today's teaching and active engagement.

COMMON CORE STATE STANDARDS: W.K.2, W.K.5, W.1.2, RI.K.1, SL.K.1, SL.K.4, SL.K.5, L.K.1.e,f; L.K.2

SAMPLE BEND

Writers Use What They Already Know

Touching and Telling the Steps across the Pages

CONNECTION

Today, call children to the meeting area with writing folders in hand. If this is new to your class, ask the children to sit on top of their folders to reduce distraction. Remind children of the list they made about how-to writing, and then read another piece and ask them to check whether it matches those descriptors.

"Writers, remember at the end of yesterday's writing workshop, when we studied *My First Soccer Game*, you made a chart listing what you noticed about how-to writing?

"I'm going to read a piece of writing that a writer in another class wrote, and I want you and your partner to notice whether this piece of how-to writing has all these things." I reread the chart.

"Ready?" I held up a book, reading the cover title: "How to Play Kickball." "The author of this book is Cooper Loval." Then, turning pages, I read:

Step 1–Make sure you make the teams.

Step 2–When the ball comes, kick it. If someone catches you ball you're OUT! But if no one catches your ball you're safe!

Step 3–When it is three outs go in the field to catch a ball.

Step 4–If you catch a ball the other person is out!

Step 5–Good catch. Thanks.

(See Figure 2–1.)

◆ COACHING

Anchor charts are meant to be referred to again and again. They should become an active teaching tool and not merely decoration for the walls of your classroom.

How-To Writing

1. Tells what to do, in steps.

2. Numbers the steps.

3. Has a picture for each step.

You can substitute a different example of how-to writing here, if you wish. It is helpful to find examples on topics that are familiar to the children, making it easier for them to understand the content.

12

GRADE K: HOW-TO BOOKS

24

Sample pages from Kindergarten, Unit 3, *How-To Books: Writing to Teach Others* — Bend I: "Writing How-To Books, Step by Step"

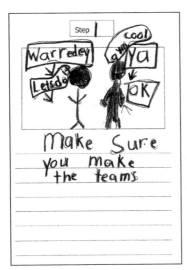

Step 1

Make Sure you make the teams

Step 2

Wen the Ball coms kick it if some one cathchis your Ball your Out! But if no wun cathchis your ball your Safe!

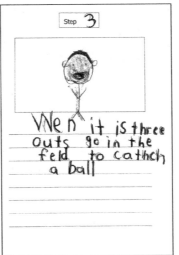

Step 3

Wen it is three outs go in the feld to cathch a ball

Step 4

if you catch a ball the ather pus in is Out!

Step 5

good catch thanks

FIG. 2–1 Cooper writes his steps across pages, numbering each step, and includes a picture for each step. He also does more, including warnings, dialogue bubbles, and sentence variety. For now, you don't need to highlight everything—save some for later in the unit.

SESSION 2: WRITERS USE WHAT THEY ALREADY KNOW

13

"Did this tell what to do, in steps? Thumbs up or thumbs down. Did Cooper number the steps? Did he include a picture for each step?" The children agreed he had done these things.

Ask children to contrast the book *they* wrote the previous day to the list of descriptors, encouraging them to revise today so their book fits the bill as a how-to book.

"Right now, please look at the book *you* wrote yesterday, and see if you already did the things on our chart, or if those are things you are going to do today." I gave them time to do this.

"Can I see thumbs up for how many of you *already* put the first step, then the next, then the next in your first how-to book?" Many children gestured thumbs up that they had done this already. "Today you can fix up or finish yesterday's book and write a new how-to book! Who knows what you will teach people to do today? Tell each other your ideas."

After a moment of buzz, I said, "Terrific. If I take your books home tonight, I'll learn how to make brownies and to play basketball and to ride a scooter and to make a friend! I'm going to have a busy night!"

❖ **Name the teaching point.**

"Today I want to teach you that when you write a how-to book, there are *new* things to do," and I gestured to the how-to chart, "but it also helps to use some of the *old* techniques you *already* learned when you were writing stories. You *still* say what you are going to write across the pages—touch and tell—and you *still* draw the pictures, saying the words that go with a picture. Only this time, each picture and page is another step."

TEACHING

While writing a class text, demonstrate how to make a how-to text, first coming up with a topic, then saying each step while touching one page at a time, and then sketching.

"Let's write a how-to book together, about something we all know how to do, so that we can practice touching and telling with how-to writing, because before now we only did that with stories. I was thinking that all of us know how to have a fire drill, because we had one just the other day. So let's get out how-to paper and remember that we first touch and tell, only this time we are telling what to do, in steps. Watch how I touch and tell the first steps of a fire drill, and then you can touch and tell the next steps."

I put my hand on my chin and pondered for a moment. "I better first remember how the fire drill goes." I looked up in the air, pulling a memory from the sky, and then, as I recalled the sequence silently to myself, I registered each step on another finger. I took hold of an enlarged chart paper booklet, touched the first page and wrote-in-the-air "How to Have a Fire Drill." Then I touched the next page and said, "Step 1. When the bells ring, it is time for a fire drill." Moving to the next page, I said, "Step 2. Then you get your jacket and get in line."

This connection is highly engaging: rather than simply looking at a text, children are asked to be active by giving a thumbs-up and by talking briefly with a partner. These added levels of scaffolding are helpful when children need extra support with new or challenging information.

Sharing and mentioning a variety of kinds of how-to books helps. If you only highlight how-to books about sports, then you are more likely to see only sports books, and the same holds for other topics.

It's helpful to use expression in your voice, as well as gestures, to emphasize the language, "Step 1 . . . step 2 . . ." Putting the emphasis on this language will help your children hear and understand that this type of writing is different than writing a narrative.

14

GRADE K: HOW-TO BOOKS

26   Sample pages from Kindergarten, Unit 3, *How-To Books: Writing to Teach Others* — Bend I: "Writing How-To Books, Step by Step"

Debrief. Name what you just did as a writer.

"Writers, did you see how I named the first steps in the fire drill, just touching the page and telling what I would write on that page? I used touch and tell, just like we used that strategy for true stories about small moments."

ACTIVE ENGAGEMENT

Invite writers to add the last couple of steps to the class how-to book, writing-in-the-air on imaginary booklets.

"Writers, it's your turn now to try doing the same for a few of the steps. Can you tell your partner what could be the next steps that you can add to our 'How to Have a Fire Drill' book? Partner 1, pretend you are holding a booklet, and turn the pages back to the very, very start of your imaginary booklet." I waited. "Are you on the title page? Starting with the title, tell all the steps, including the ones we just said, and then keep going, past where I stopped. Do all the steps 'til you get to the class standing outside, okay? Partner 1, hold your imaginary booklet, point to the cover, and start!"

As I approached Sofia, she was saying to Preston, "Step 4. You walk outside and line up across the street."

To the whole class, I said, "Once you've touched and told up to the part where the class is outside, pass the imaginary booklet to your partner and let Partner 2 give the steps for coming back inside."

Preston pretended to touch the page and said, "Next, listen for the whistle and come back in the school." I moved quickly to listen in to other partnerships.

LINK

Remind writers that after rehearsing the entire booklet, they go back to page 1, sketch, and write.

"Writers, when you are writing, after you touch and tell the pages, you will want to go back to page one and touch that page, say the words to yourself, and then draw the picture for that step. Remember, as you draw the picture, it helps to say in your mind what you will write!"

I wrote "1" in the box at the top of the first page and then quickly made a sketch for the first step, saying the words as I did this, and then quickly wrote the words.

"Writers, we all just worked together on 'How to Have a Fire Drill,' but does that mean you all have to write a how-to book about fire drills? No! Of course not! You can write a book that teaches people to do anything you know how to do. Thumbs up if you have your idea for what you will teach in today's how-to book." The children signaled. "Thumbs up if you are ready to touch and tell your own how-to book across the pages?" Again, most signaled yes. "Fantastic. There are new booklets waiting for you in baskets at each of your tables. Some of you may still need to finish yesterday's book, so do that first. As soon as you get back to your writing spot, you can get started! Off you go."

Imaginary booklets are quick and ready to go, with no additional materials for children to manage at the meeting area. (Remember, they are already sitting on their writing folders.) An alternative would be to provide blank booklets, as a more tactile way to practice today's work.

15

Varying Small-Group Methods and Structures

YOU SAY TO THE KIDS, "Off you go!" and of course, it's not only the kids who get started. You do as well. For a moment, you'll want to just watch as they make their way from the meeting area to their work places. Be mindful that this is a moment for you to do some important assessment. By this point in the year, all your children should be able to make the transition from the meeting area to their writing places, from listening to writing, without needing an intervention. If they seem to need you to run from one child to another, giving individual jump starts, that's a problem.

So watch them get started, and if you see that there are many in the classroom who have become so dependent on you that they just sit at their writing spots, waiting for you to get to them and say, "What are you going to write?" and then, "Great, put that down," then you'll want to decide on some actions to take to support greater independence. That action can provide more or less scaffolding. The least scaffolded response would be a voiceover, delivered to the whole class as children work (or don't work, as the case may be). "Writers, I should see all of you rereading what you wrote yesterday and then either finishing that book or starting on a new one." Another way to nudge writers to get started is to move quickly among the children, using nonverbal cues to signal, "Get started." A tap on one child's page, a gesture that says, "Get writing" delivered to another, a firm "Now" to a third.

If children need yet more help, you might try table conferences. Pull up a chair alongside a table full of writers, and be sure they do not stop to talk to you but instead continue their work. "Just ignore me and get going. I want to study the way you work," you can say, holding your clipboard at the ready. If few actually are working, then you probably want a small-group conversation. "Writers, I'm confused. Why aren't you writing?" The conversation may need to become a little lesson on getting yourself started in your writing.

Once all your writers are writing, you'll be able to decide what to do. It can help to quickly consider your options. Do you want to confer individually or lead small groups? If you feel that many kids are needing some help, choose the latter. Then you can think,

MID-WORKSHOP TEACHING Writers Need Not Sound Out Every Word; Some Words They Know in a Snap

"Writers, I love seeing that some of you are remembering that you don't need to stretch out every word. Some words you just know in a snap. Like, let's say you want to write that when the fire drill bell rings, you stand *in* line. Right now, with your finger-pen, write *in* on your hand.

"How many of you said, '*In*. I know *in*,' and you just wrote it? Good for you. And did some of you say, '*In*. That's on our word wall,' and glance up at the word wall? Good for you! As you keep working, I know you'll be stretching some words out. And other words, you'll know in a snap!"

As Students Continue Working . . .

"Don't forget to reread your writing, and ask yourself, 'Will someone else be able to read this?'"

"Writers, I love all the different how-to books I am seeing. Listen to some of them: 'How to Set the Table,' 'How to Play Laser Tag,' 'How to Ice Skate,' 'How to Make Hot Chocolate.' And there are many more. Can you believe how many things we will be able to do after we read each other's how-to books?"

"Can I tell you about a problem that Jennifer solved by working hard at it? She is writing a book about how to be a good friend. She didn't have enough paper for her steps, so she went to the writing center, got two more sheets of paper, took apart her booklet, added in more paper, wrote her two more steps, and then stapled her book back together! Good problem-solving work, right?"

16

GRADE K: HOW-TO BOOKS

28

Sample pages from Kindergarten, Unit 3, *How-To Books: Writing to Teach Others* — Bend I: "Writing How-To Books, Step by Step"

"What are four or five possible topics I could teach in small groups?" Or you can think, "What are several possible methods I could use to lead small groups?"

Let's say you decide to go with some different methods. You should have a bunch of these at your fingertips. For example, one method for teaching a small group is to confer with one child and then gather a group of kids together to say, "Can I show you what so-and-so just did that some of the rest of you might try?" Then you need to story-tell the sequential story of what you helped the one child to do, only we generally take ourselves out of that story so that instead of saying, "Then I told her to reread her writing," say, "Then she decided she'd reread her writing."

A second method for leading small groups revolves around the use of a mentor text. You can convene a group of writers and say, "One of the things that I do a lot as a writer, and I know most writers do, is that I study examples of the kind of writing I'm trying to make. So I thought maybe the group of us could study this how-to book, and you guys could try to figure out some things *you* could do to make your books really, really special."

Another way of leading small groups may involve treating these as essentially peer-response groups. You could gather several partnerships and set children up to alternate reading their writing aloud and giving each other feedback. If you decide to do so, you could channel children to give feedback on specific things, such as on each other's teaching pictures or on the clarity of the directions. You could, over time, work with children so that they anticipate that when you listen to their small group or partner conversations, you'll use gestures to signal ways they can improve the conversations. You can teach them that whenever you point to the paper, this is meant as a signal for them to reference the writing more exactly. When you point to a person other than the speaker, this is a signal to let that other person join into the conversation. Children, of course, will enjoy helping you devise signals for all that you might want to say to a small group, and in doing so, they rehearse ways to improve their conversations.

Then, too, small groups can be designed as inquiry groups, with writers bringing their work to the group and expecting to lay their work out and study what they have done and what others have done. When doing this, students can look across the work that several children did, identifying an instance where one writer did one thing or another especially well, and they can talk about what made that work exemplary. Of course, the natural next step is for children to help each other emulate the successful model.

Checking Writing against the Anchor Chart

Remind writers that earlier they had looked at student writing to see ways it aligned to the list of characteristics of how-to writing. Do this again, with the day's new writing.

"Writers, earlier today we looked at Cooper's book to see whether it had all the characteristics of the how-to writing we studied. Look at the new writing you did today, and see if it matches all that we have observed about how-to writing. As I read each item from our chart, will you and your partner point to places in your writing where you did that item from our chart? And if you haven't *yet* done some of this, you can work together to do it now." I then read from this list, pausing between each item."

> ### How-To Writing
>
> 1. Tells what to do, in steps.
>
> 2. Numbers the steps.
>
> 3. Has a picture for each step.

As children reread their how-to books to check for each item on the chart, I stood up from my chair to read over their shoulders. I made a short list of things that I noticed could use improving. Once we'd moved through all three items on the chart, I said:

"You are really thinking like writers now, rereading your own work! Now, I noticed that almost everybody had steps and numbers, and almost everybody had pictures for each step, BUT I also noticed that sometimes the pictures didn't really show much action. For example, look at Cooper Loval's book again. See how the people in his pictures are just standing there? You can't really tell what they are doing, can you? I think it would help a lot if every picture actually showed what the people were doing, don't you? Writers, right now, will you add to one of your pictures to make sure that really shows exactly what is happening? Try moving the arms or legs, add objects if you need to, or draw where the person is. You should probably use labels, too, to help us learn from your pictures."

The share is an opportunity to deepen the work that children have done so far. Yes, nearly all your children will be drawing and/or writing steps by now. But with how much detail? And did they reread their work to make sure it all makes sense? You can adapt this share session to highlight work that your particular students will benefit from.

18

GRADE K: HOW-TO BOOKS

30   *Sample pages from Kindergarten, Unit 3, How-To Books: Writing to Teach Others* — Bend I: "Writing How-To Books, Step by Step"

Writers Become Readers, Asking, "Can I Follow This?"

THINK FOR A MOMENT about the way you learn skills, for example, the skills you have been learning about teaching writing as you work through these books. Presumably, when you started the first few sessions of the first book, you taught a full writing workshop. You gathered children, gave them a minilesson, sent them off to write, worked with individuals and small groups, and then convened the children. Now you continue to do all those things, but thinking about writing instruction is much more nuanced. You are aware of the differences between minilessons in which you use your writing as an example and those in which you rely on a child's piece of writing. You are aware that sometimes a minilesson ends with children getting started writing while they are still on the rug, and sometimes you send children off to work on their writing. And so on.

"This minilesson is the cornerstone of the unit. Prepare yourself to have a lot of fun, to let your children collapse into giggles."

In the same way, children will have been using fundamental skills repeatedly. For example, a month or so ago, at the start of the *Writing for Readers* unit, children learned that writers reread. They learned that writers use one end of the pencil to write, then flip the pencil over and use the other end of the pencil as a pointer to help with reading. Today you return to the concept that writers reread, only this time, your focus is less on the word work of rereading one's own writing and more on the work of comprehension and monitoring for sense, and you will teach the specific ways writers reread how-to writing.

This is a favorite minilesson. It was a mainstay in the first edition of Units of Study for Primary Writing. In many ways, it is the cornerstone of this unit. Enjoy it. Prepare yourself to have a lot of fun, to let your children collapse into giggles.

IN THIS SESSION, you'll teach students that writers reread their writing as they go, making changes along the way.

GETTING READY

✔ An example of student writing, displayed for the class to see (see Connection)

✔ Students' writing folders, from the previous session, and pencils (see Connection)

✔ An example of student how-to writing whose steps are unclear or difficult to follow (see Teaching)

✔ Chart paper and markers for rewriting part of a how-to booklet (see Active Engagement)

✔ Successful (easy to follow) how-to writing by one child in the class that he or she will read during the share

✔ "How-To Writing" anchor chart from previous sessions on display

COMMON CORE STATE STANDARDS: W.K.2, W.K.5, RI.K.1, RI.K.2, RFS.K.1, RFS.K.2, SL.K.1, SL.K.2, SL.K.3, SL.K.6, L.K.1, L.K.2

19

SAMPLE BEND

Writers Become Readers, Asking, "Can I Follow This?"

CONNECTION

Celebrate one child who reread her how-to book, reminding all students of the importance of rereading.

"Writers, yesterday I saw Sofia writing her how-to book, and do you know what she did? She wrote one of her steps, and then after she wrote that step, that page, she flipped her magic pencil over to the other end and used it as a pointer to help her reread her writing.

"Sofia, I've got your book displayed on the easel. Can you come up and show the class how you reread your writing?" Sofia scrambled up to the front of the meeting area and used her pencil's eraser to tap out her words. (See Figure 3–1 on p. 21.)

Step 1–First take the cover and pull up. Make sure you hold with two hands.

Step 2–Then you smooth it out to make it smoother.

Step 3–Next take the blanket and pull it up with two hands.

Step 4–Then put the pillow up with two hands. Stuff it up.

Step 5–Put the stuffed animal on.

"Writers, you see how Sofia crossed words out and added in more words? What happened is that she reread her book and realized, 'Hey, wait a minute. I could say more!' Then she added the missing parts. That's good work, Sofia, to remember what you learned earlier about writers needing to become readers and about revision. You remembered that work from when you were working on your true stories last month!"

Bring home the importance of rereading by asking students to reread their writing from the day before, making small revisions as they go.

"Right now, will each of you get out the books you wrote yesterday? Use the eraser end of your pencils to reread just a page of your books, for now, and then if something is missing, do like Sofia did, and flip your pencils back to the writing end and fix things up."

You may have noticed that in minilessons where students will use a piece of their own writing, we usually ask them to bring their entire writing folder to the meeting area, even when only one booklet is needed. Many teachers find that a consistent routine for bringing work to the meeting area helps to move things along and avoids confusion. Alternatively, you could direct children to bring one how-to booklet instead of the entire folder.

There are many different ways you can have students share their writing during a minilesson. Sometimes it is enough for a student to just read her writing aloud. However, in this instance, it was important that the rest of the class actually see Sofia's writing, as well as the way she used her eraser to tap out the words as she read. Pages can be pulled apart and displayed side by side. Or if you have a document camera, simply use that to enlarge the writing.

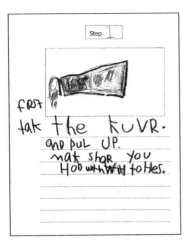

Step 1

frst
tak the kuvr.
and pul up.
nat shor you
hob with with to has.

Step 2

Then Yoo Smovr
It dfoutto
may it smovr.

Step 3

Next tam
the bluth any
plitup wihto has.

Step 4

staft it up.
is put the plow
up with to has.
stuf it up.

FIG. 3–1 Sofia revises her book on how to make a bed by simply crossing out the parts she'd like to change.

Step 5

Put the
stoft enome
on if you

For a moment, children worked. I signaled that those who finished before the others could move on to their second pages.

❖ **Name the teaching point.**

"Today I want to teach you that how-to writers don't just reread the words, touching them with a finger or a pencil. How-to writers *also* reread to check that their writing makes sense. To do that kind of rereading, writers reread to a partner or to themselves and make sure it is easy to follow the steps.

TEACHING

Demonstrate what it means to check your directions with a partner, noticing whether the directions make sense or need to be revised for clarity.

"The best way to check whether your directions will make sense is to read them to someone who will try to follow the steps, to do whatever you are teaching (for real or for pretend). If the partner can't figure out what you mean, if he or she can't figure out what to do, that means your directions don't *quite* work, and then you can revise them.

"Let's try reading the words of one of your books and see if we can follow those words, okay? Sam is writing a how-to book on doing a somersault. He'll read it to me, and let's all see if I can follow his directions." I brought Sam to sit on a chair beside my chair.

SESSION 3: WRITERS BECOME READERS, ASKING, "CAN I FOLLOW THIS?"

21

SAMPLE BEND

"Sam will read me his book (just the start—it isn't done), and I'll do whatever his book tells me to do. Writers, when you do this kind of reading—when you read directions—instead of reading the book straight through, it helps to read one step and then do that step, then read the next step, and then do that step."

Sam read, "First put your head down and your legs up." I looked at him, as if asking *What?* He reread, "First put your head down," and, still sitting on a chair at the front of the meeting area, I tucked my chin toward my chest. Then Sam read, "And your legs up." (Remember, I was still on the chair!) "Okay, my head is down, but hmm, my legs go up? To somersault?" I raised my feet so they stuck straight out from the chair. A bit puzzled, I said, "Okay, keep reading."

Sam had by now covered his eyes in dismay, though we could all see his huge grin. He read his next page, starting to giggle: "Then turn over."

"Turn over? I'll hurt myself!"

When the writer of confusing directions makes verbal revisions, capitalize on this, and name that, yes, after checking for clarity, writers often revise.

Sam started to protest that when he had told me to put my head down, he meant I needed to put my head *on the floor* and that of course I needed to get off the chair to do so, but I returned to the role of teacher rather than gymnast to be. "Are you saying, Sam, that now you realize you need to make revisions to your directions?" When he nodded vigorously, I said, "That's what happens when you reread your writing to a partner and see the way that person struggles to follow what you have written."

ACTIVE ENGAGEMENT

Ask children to think with their partners about ways to revise the original instructions. Attempt to follow the revised instructions, highlighting the idea that being specific makes directions easier to follow.

"Tell your partner how you might start a book on doing somersaults that could maybe work better," I said, and the room erupted into conversation.

Convening the class, I called, "Okay, let's try out another set of directions for doing a somersault. Just tell me the new steps, and I'll follow them."

This time the first step was "Sit on the floor."

"Okay, first you sit on the floor." After I clamored off the chair, I wrote on a piece of chart paper, "1. First, sit on the floor." "Okay, I've done that. What's next?"

"Put your head on the floor." I touched my face to the floor, not putting my head in the proper position.

22

34

Sample pages from Kindergarten, Unit 3, *How-To Books: Writing to Teach Others* — Bend I: "Writing How-To Books, Step by Step"

Another child called, "No! Put the *top* of your head . . ."

I pointed out, "That's a smart revision! Put *the top of your head* on the floor." On the chart paper, I wrote, "2. Put the top of your head on the floor."

"You are getting better at realizing the details your readers will need. We'll stop here for now. This is such smart work! You are thinking about your readers and writing steps that will help them."

LINK

Tell children they'll need to decide what they will do, knowing many will recruit a partner to help them reread to check that the partner can follow the text.

"Writers, writing time is really your work time. Today as you work, think about everything you have learned so far." I gestured to our anchor chart to remind children of some of the key points. "You can be the boss of writing time and decide what you need to do to be sure you have a whole folder full of great how-to writing. Let's just think about what you *could* decide to do today. Who has an idea of what you could do?"

Sam suggested, "I could write an *even better* book on somersaults and headstands too 'cause I know how to do them."

I nodded, agreeing that writers could write whole new books. "And if you do that, write the directions so I won't fall and break my head, okay? So you might write whole new books. What else might you do today?"

One writer piped in with "Reread?" I practically fell off my chair over the brilliance of her suggestion. "You aren't going to need a teacher anymore. You are learning to teach yourselves. How totally cool that you take the stuff we did with Sam's book and imagine doing it with your own books. Do you mean you might bring your book to someone in the class and say, 'Will you try to do what I say?' and then watch whether they get as confused as I did?" The children nodded vigorously.

"Might you even *revise* your book to make it clearer? That would be *so* grown-up." The kids were definite that they'd absolutely do that.

"Oh my goodness. So get going. Don't waste a second. I gotta see this."

Session 3: Writers Become Readers, Asking, "Can I Follow This?"

23

Anticipating that Some Children Will Need Scaffolds and Supports to Access High-Level Work

THE MOST PRESSING THING YOU WILL NOTICE TODAY is that some children will quite rightly tell you they can't follow each other's directions. "I can't ski in this room, can I?" they'll say. You will need to show children that they can read each other's directions and *imagine* following them. If the directions say, "Break an egg on the edge of the bowl," the reader can grasp an imaginary egg and break it on the edge of the imaginary bowl. If the directions say, "When the person in line in front of you gets on the ski lift, push yourself forward quickly so that you are standing in the place where the lift will get you," then perhaps the actor is a finger puppet made from your two fingers, who pushes forward on imaginary skis. The important thing to realize is that the process of reading directions is a stop and go activity. The reader reads a step, then does the step—really doing it or imagining doing it. Then the reader presses on, reading the next step. This sort of reading can be done in a way that reveals potential problems in a draft.

While children read their how-to writing to each other and work to address the problems they see, you will want to also read their writing and think about how you can address the problems *you* see. Whereas the kids will address problems by adding words to their pages, you'll address problems with small-group work, mid-workshop teaching points, and minilessons you write on your own to address issues that we never imagined.

For example, if you find that your children are choosing topics such as "when I went to my grandma's house" that don't set them up to write procedural pieces, then you will want to spend more time immersing them in the sounds of procedural writing. This means it will be important for you to read how-to writing aloud. Don't talk this reading to death. Just read and immerse your children in the language of the genre. Meanwhile, find opportunities to give the class oral directions. "Today we're going to make bracelets. Let me teach you how. Listen. I'm going to give you all the how-to directions now. You'll see my directions will be like a how-to book. First, you . . ." Meanwhile, help children develop lists of topics that match the genre and key phrases they can use at the start of these texts that help to angle their writing. For example, you might have these words, hanging prominently in your classroom: "Do you want to know how to . . . ? I will teach you. First you . . ."

MID-WORKSHOP TEACHING **Writers Say It a Different Way if a Partner Doesn't Understand**

Near the end of writing time, I spoke up loudly, getting the children's attention. "Writers," I said, "eyes on me. When you read the directions from your how-to book to your partner, and your partner says, 'Wait, I'm confused. I can't follow these directions,' that's your signal that you have to do something. Do you just leave it the way it is and go on? No! Of course not. Here's a tip: try saying it a different way, and then ask your partner, 'Does it make sense now?' Then take your pen and cross out the old writing and put in the new way of saying whatever was confusing."

It may be that in your class there are one or two children that need extra special help getting started. Perhaps these are children who are just learning to speak English, or perhaps these are children who are extremely reluctant to take risks for fear of getting it wrong. In any case, the heaviest scaffolding you could provide might be to offer up the class how-to book to these few individuals to write as their own. You might say, "Remember how we wrote 'How to Have a Fire Drill' together yesterday? Well, guess what? The kids who come to this school next year are not going to know how to have a fire drill, and it would be great to have that written as a book. Would you each be willing to write that book for them? You could help each other." By offering each child a blank booklet and encouraging them to say those familiar fire drill steps aloud, you're helping them transfer familiar language and vocabulary from one context (whole-class, shared writing) to another (on their own in a small booklet). Encourage them to put it in their own words and draw their own pictures now that they have their own small booklet to write "How to Have a Fire Drill." As soon as they are up and running, leave them to continue, not without letting them know that they can write their next how-to book on any topic they choose!

24

GRADE K: HOW-TO BOOKS

Envisioning the Steps in a How-To Book and Revising if They Don't Make Sense

Ask children to join you in listening and mentally following one child's directions.

"Today I saw something really terrific. Listen to this. I saw many of you reading directions not only to your partner, *but also to yourselves*! You reread what you wrote and thought, 'If I follow my own directions, will they work?' I have asked Nicole to read her how-to book to us. As she reads, let's close our eyes and see if we can picture ourselves doing each of these steps."

Nicole read her writing.

> Nicole
>
> How to Plant a Flower
>
> 1. First dig a hole. Then put the seeds in the hole.
>
> 2. Cover the hole with dirt. Water your flowers.
>
> 3. Then give your flower some sunlight and take care of your flower.
>
> 4. Talk to your flower. Then your flower will grow.

Nicole hadn't yet finished the book, but she told her classmates what she planned to write on the final page: "One day it will start to grow." "Thumbs up if you were able to see the steps of that happening." Thumbs went up across the room. "I feel ready to plant a flower right now!"

Ask children to turn to their partners and read aloud. The listener will try to imagine doing the steps.

"Writers, would you get with your partners? Partner 1, read your book to Partner 2, just like Nicole read her book to us. And Partner 1, listen and see if you can picture yourself doing each step. Are the directions clear? Do you know what to do first and next and next?"

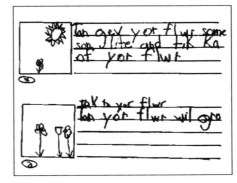

FIG. 3–2   Nicole's writing is easy to follow, in part because she writes more than one sentence for each step. This simple strategy could be tucked into small-group, conferring, or even a mid-workshop teaching point or share.

SESSION 3: WRITERS BECOME READERS, ASKING, "CAN I FOLLOW THIS?"

25

SAMPLE BEND

I listened in as Troyquon turned to his partner, Rachel, and began to read:

A Cook Book How to Make Pizza

Step One: Throw up the dough.

Step Two: Spin the dough in your fingers.

Stept Three: Pat the dough into a flat circle.

Step Four: Put tomatoes onto the dough.
　　　　　Put the dough into the pan.

Rachel interrupted after Troyquon read Step Three. "A flat circle? How will it look like a pizza, not a donut?"

Help writers realize that if listeners aren't able to follow the steps in a how-to book, revision is necessary.

I agreed. "Rachel is asking a good question. That's so helpful, isn't it Troyquon? With that help, you can go back and reread and think, 'Have I told her enough?'"

Troyquon looked dubious about reconsidering his text, and it was time for the share session to end. Seizing the moment, I said, "I'll tell you what—why don't I take your directions home and try following them. I'd love to eat some pizza tonight!"

Troyquon took a sticky note and carefully wrote his telephone number. "If you need me, call me."

I convened the class. "Class, I'm going to follow Troyquon's pizza recipe tonight. I have a Post-it with his phone number in case it doesn't work. Will you listen and tell me if you think I'll need to call him?" I read Troyquon's piece to the class. "Thumbs up if you think I'll need to call him." Most of the kids raised their thumbs. "Hmm. Well, I'll give it a try and let all of you know tomorrow if I get stuck!" I made a mental note to follow up with this during morning meeting the next day.

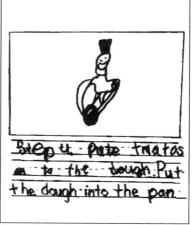

FIG. 3–3　Troyquon's pictures are nearly as helpful as the words for readers to understand his directions.

26

GRADE K: HOW-TO BOOKS

38　　　Sample pages from Kindergarten, Unit 3, *How-To Books: Writing to Teach Others* — Bend I: "Writing How-To Books, Step by Step"

Writers Answer a Partner's Questions

TRY WRITING IN A WAY that allows someone else to learn from you. You'll find it is not easy! Certainly you have found times when this book is not as clear as you wish it were. "Huh?" you ask. "What are you saying?"

It is especially challenging for a five- or six-year-old to write clear directions for someone else because children at this age are egocentric. They tend to see the world through their own eyes and not imagine that others see something different. It was but a few years ago when these children were toddlers who would cover their eyes up and say, "You can't see me." They'd be standing in full view in front of us, but because their eyes were covered and they couldn't see us, they assumed that in fact *they* were invisible!

It is a very big deal, then, to ask children to write in ways that take into account what others need to know to fully comprehend a message. The words of your minilesson won't be enough to make children able to imagine another person's perspective. Instead, you will want to use your minilesson to channel children to engage in repeated practice, doing the sorts of things that will (after repeated practice) eventually allow them to walk in the shoes of someone else—in this case, a reader.

The great news is that you have the one most important scaffold for this sort of intellectual education right at hand: a partner. The great psychologist Lev Vygotsky had it right when he suggested that learners can first do with the help of someone else what they can eventually do on their own. The goal of today's minilesson, then, is not so much to inform students about a new concept as to create for them another opportunity to experience another person's perspective.

IN THIS SESSION, you'll teach students that writing partners help each other make how-to books clearer and easier to follow.

GETTING READY

✔ An enlarged version of the text used for demonstration in Session 2 ("How to Have a Fire Drill") (see Connection)

✔ A loaf of bread, jars of peanut butter and jelly, a plate, and a plastic knife or spoon (see Teaching)

✔ A book you have written on how to make a peanut butter and jelly sandwich (which you'll pretend to have found on your desk that morning). Include the following steps, deliberately leaving the directions open to misunderstanding) (see Teaching).

1. Get the jar of peanut butter.
2. Put it on the bread.
3. Now get the jelly.

✔ "How-To Writing" anchor chart from previous sessions on display (see Mid-Workshop Teaching)

COMMON CORE STATE STANDARDS: W.K.2, W.K.5, RI.K.1, SL.K.1.a, SL.K.2, SL.K.3, SL.K.6, L.K.1.d, L.K.1, L.K.2

SAMPLE BEND

Writers Answer a Partner's Questions

CONNECTION

Once you have a captive audience, reread the class how-to book aloud. This provides a novel way to remind children of relevant prior instruction.

When the children gathered, I made myself busy rereading our class how-to book, "How to Have a Fire Drill." I first flipped my pencil around and used the eraser end to reread, pointing to each word, fixing up a small thing or two as I reread. Then I started to reread a second time, acting out the steps as I read them. Partway through this, I feigned finally noticing that the kids were all waiting for me.

"Oh, so sorry. I didn't notice that you were all here. I was so busy rereading. Readers, I know some of you have been rereading your how-to books too. How many of you have reread them with your magic pencil, touching each word and fixing things up if you see that you left something out?" The children signaled that they had, and I nodded, then added, "How many of you reread your book to someone else, checking to see if they could follow your directions?" Again, many children signaled that they had done that.

Name the teaching point.

"Well, today I want to tell you that writers feel really lucky if they have readers who not only try to follow their directions, but who also speak up, saying things like 'I'm confused' or 'Can you explain that more clearly?' when they need to do so."

TEACHING

Remind students that writing partners are wonderful helpers.

"Have you ever noticed that inside many books there is a section where the writer says, 'My thanks go to so-and-so, who helped me with this book.' Some of you are probably going to end up wanting to write one of those thank-you sections inside the cover of some of your books, because your partner is a really good writing helper.

◆ COACHING

By modeling for the class how I reread with my magic pencil, making revisions as I go, I am showing them that these habits are a way of life. All writers reread their writing and make revisions. It's not enough for us to simply tell children to do it—we need to show them how we do it, too.

28

GRADE K: HOW-TO BOOKS

40   Sample pages from Kindergarten, Unit 3, *How-To Books: Writing to Teach Others* — Bend I: "Writing How-To Books, Step by Step"

"I've written a book that I want to put in the school library for all the kids to read, but it isn't quite finished yet. I was hoping you could all help me finish it today. I'm going to show you how to be a helper for me, so that you can be great helpers for each other."

Recruit a child to play the role of your writing partner. Coach the child to act out the steps of a how-to book and give suggestions for making it stronger.

"But before I ask for everybody's help, I would really love a partner, a helper, who tries to follow my directions and who also has the courage to tell me (nicely) places where my book is a little confusing. Would one of you be willing to be my writing partner?"

I soon had a partner, Julissa, sitting next to me at the front of the room. "I'll read the book to you. Do you want to follow it in your mind or for real (because my book is one you could do for real)"? My partner shrugged, unclear, so I laid the loaf of bread, jars of peanut butter and jelly, plate, and plastic knife I'd earlier tucked behind my chair before them. "Okay, I'll read my steps, you follow the steps—and tell me if you are ever confused."

Then I said to the rest of the class, "Julissa is my writing partner right now, but all of you can join along. Will you all pretend you have an imaginary loaf of bread, and imaginary jars of peanut butter and jelly in front of you and try following this book too?"

Then I read (hoping to confuse the kids).

1. Get the jar of peanut butter.
2. Put it on the bread. (I expect kids to put the jar on the loaf.)
3. Now get the jelly.

By now, some kids were laughing. I looked startled. "What are you saying? My directions weren't clear enough for you?"

Tell students that writers use their partners' feedback to revise their books for clarity.

The kids let on that the directions were confusing. "What?" I asked. "Julissa, you are my writing partner. You will tell me the truth, right? Does my how-to teach you all the steps? Does it make sense?" Julissa giggled and said, "No, it doesn't. You told us to put the *jar* on the bread!"

I pretended that this was a major realization for me. "Oh, I see. It is confusing. Let me try those directions again, changing them to clear up your confusion."

When we teach people to do something—to swim or to teach or to write procedural texts—one of the challenges is deciding what matters. What skills do we want to be sure learners develop? It'd be easy to teach writers details about the features one finds in how-to texts. The trick is to steer our teaching away from trivial pursuits! Here, we have decided that we want children to grasp the idea that how-to books are written for readers with sequenced, clear directions.

Be sure to choose a topic that is meaningful and familiar to your students. Whether you decide to write "How to Clean a Guinea Pig Cage" or "How to Make Chocolate Pudding," the essence of this lesson is the same.

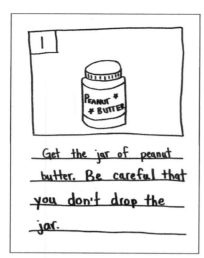

FIG. 4–1   This chart-sized how-to book will become a shared text the class adds to throughout the unit. Using the method of shared writing, the kids will contribute the ideas for the writing, and the teacher will take the role of scribe (though we often restate or add to children's contributions as we go). Thus the shared text that is created is a joint effort, a collaboration between teacher and students.

This time, the kids had more success. I paused. "I'm not going to finish all these directions, but I just have to tell you that tonight, I'm going to add a new section to my book. I'm going to say, 'My thanks go to my writing partner and my readers, who helped me know parts of my first draft that were confusing.' Thanks so much for helping me.

"Writers, did you see how helpful it was to have a partner who was brave and honest with me. She let me know that my writing was confusing and I needed to explain things more clearly, didn't she?"

ACTIVE ENGAGEMENT

Ask students to generate ideas about how to be helpful partners.

Julissa returned to her seat to join the class. "Writers, right now turn to your partner to talk about ways you can be even more helpful to each other."

The room erupted in conversation, and I listened in. Lexi was in the middle of her conversation with Oliver. "You are a good partner when you tell me I left out a word. 'Cause I said 'I poured the into Daisy's bowl,' and I forgot to write 'dog food.'"

30

Oliver nodded. "*And* tell Daisy is a dog. 'Cause they might think it is your *sister* eating dog food!" The two pantomimed eating yucky dog food, and I noted to myself that at some point I'd tell them that laughing together also makes for a good partnership.

LINK

Remind children that they'll not only get suggestions from partners, but they'll also revise to respond to those suggestions.

"Today when you are with your partner, you can listen closely to your partner's how-to book and really act it out, step by step. When you aren't quite sure what to do to act it out, ask your partner to say more. You could say, 'What do I need to do next?' or 'I'm confused. Can you say more?'

"The important thing will not just be to listen to a partner's questions and confusions, but also to realize that when the partner is confused, that is a signal that you need to revise your book to make it clear. How many of you remember about adding extra pages to a book?" They signaled yes. "How many of you think you could use arrows to squeeze more information into the right spots in your books?" Again, many signaled yes. "You can add sentences, or even whole pages to your how-to book, just like I did when you guys asked me questions!"

Create a drumroll around the upcoming end of this bend in the unit, and rally kids to start new books sometime today.

"Writers, you probably will begin by revising the books you have already written, but then you will definitely start a new book. Pretty soon, we're going to come to the end of this part of our unit, and we're going to celebrate by laying *all* your how-to books out, like in a museum. You are definitely going to want to have a whole bunch finished. So get started, quick as a wink."

If you worry that this will be an invitation to chaos, you can settle for asking writers to read directions to themselves and imagine what their readers will make of each step. But we recommend letting other kids try out the directions.

SAMPLE BEND

Conferring with Writing Partners

AS YOU'LL REMEMBER, just as minilessons follow a particular template, so, too, do conferences. At the start of a conference, you will generally want to do some quick research to learn what the writer is working on. That research usually begins with a bit of observation and listening. Of course, the observation and listening is especially easy when a writer is working with a partner, since this externalizes what children are doing and thinking. For example, when I pulled alongside Melissa and her partner, Nicole, I first listened long enough to learn that the girls were trying to figure out how to try out Melissa's directions for making chocolate lollipops. Nicole had a pout on her face, and she threw up her hands with exasperation.

"So, writers, can you fill me in on what you are doing now?" I asked.

Nicole said, "I am supposed to try Melissa's directions, but she doesn't have the chocolate, so I don't know how to do it."

Melissa responded, "I'm reading my writing and Nicole is doing my directions, but she's not doing them."

"*I can't!* I don't have the chocolate!" Nicole explained.

Listening to the two, it was of course immediately apparent to me that they were struggling a bit, but frankly, I was also pleased. It had been a day or two since I'd taught them to try out each other's and their own directions, and these two girls had initiated doing this work on their own. This made it easy to move on to the next stage of a conference, supporting the writers by naming something that they had tried.

"I can see you guys are frustrated, but you know what? You are trying to do something really smart—testing out the directions to see if they work. And the really important thing is that even though it was a few days ago when I taught you to do this, you haven't forgotten and haven't needed me to remind you that this is a strategy you can use any day. You're doing it all by yourself."

Then I added what was essentially the teaching point for this conference. "But do you remember how, in the minilesson, I said that sometimes we are going to need to *pretend* that we are following the directions? Writers have to do that a lot. When I wrote about peanut butter and jelly, I had to pretend, so I could get the exact words down."

MID-WORKSHOP TEACHING   Writers Not Only Revise Old Books; They Also Write New Books

"Writers, I'm glad you have been revising. This classroom has felt like a carpentry shop with kids taping strips of paper into their books and stapling new pages into books. Give yourselves a pat on the back if you have done some revision to make your writing even more clear for your readers.

"Although I am glad you've done some revision, I also want to remind you that you need to get started on another book. A good way to know if you are ready to start another book is to use our chart as a checklist." I pointed to our anchor chart.

How-To Writing

1. Tells what to do, in steps.

2. Numbers the steps.

3. Has a picture for each step.

Sample pages from Kindergarten, Unit 3, *How-To Books: Writing to Teach Others* — Bend I: "Writing How-To Books, Step by Step"

"If you have done all these things, then chances are, you are probably ready to start another book! For just a second, let's remember all the things that you know how to do that you could teach others. How many of you know how to do something related to sports. Like, maybe you know how to throw a Frisbee, maybe you know how to do a headstand, or maybe you know how to arm wrestle. If you know something related to a sport, you could write about that. All of you know something related to school. You know how to count and how to count by twos and how to add and take away, right? If you have little brothers or sisters, they do not know those things, and you could be their math professor. Or you could write a book teaching some little kid in your life how to read. Give me a thumbs up if you have an idea for a how-to book that you will get started on right this second." The children signaled, and I said, "Fast! We only have fifteen more minutes."

Knowing it was now time to teach, and deciding to teach through guided practice, I said, "Nicole, let's both be readers, and we'll listen to Melissa's directions and *pretend* we're making chocolate lollipops in our minds. Let's see if we can let the words help us create a picture (just like when we read about being at the ocean and create the picture). Let's try together, okay?"

Melissa began, "Melt the chocolate."

"Okay, so Nicole and I are going to pretend now. Nicole, let's do it. I held up my hands as though ready to grab something out of the air, but then stopped. I looked up into space as if trying to conjure up an image. "I'm having a hard time getting a picture in my mind. I can't make a picture of how to melt it. Do you put it in your hands like when you put snow in your hands and it melts?" Then I turned to my coreader and said,

"How about you, Nicole? Do Melissa's words tell you enough to be able to imagine how to do this?"

Nicole said, "No. How does it melt? Do you light a fire?"

"You have to put the chocolate over hot water to melt it," Melissa clarified.

"*Oh!* Now I can picture how you do it! First, you put the chocolate over the hot water and that is how you melt it," I restated the first step in Melissa's directions, adding the new information.

"Melissa, keep reading. Read the next step." As she read it, I said, "Nicole, try to imagine what her words are saying in your mind. Then you can tell Melissa what you see, and she can check whether her directions are doing the job."

Melissa continued, "Put the melted chocolate in the mold."

I looked over at Nicole to see if she seemed to be making a mental picture and asked what she was seeing. She said, "I'm pouring it in. It is spilling all over."

I gave her a thumbs up. Melissa, however, added. "Wait. You have to get a spoon and put the chocolate in the mold slowly with a spoon."

"What a smart revision you just thought of! Later you better put that down!"

By this point, it was time to end the conference, so I did as I generally do at the end of a conference. I quickly debriefed, reminding the girls of the strategy we used to link it to the writing work they would do in the future. "So, Melissa, now you need to go back and reread your first page, trying to make a movie in your mind of it—'Melt the chocolate'—and see if you can remember what you need to do differently on that first page so that readers will be able to make a movie in their minds of the whole thing. Then reread the next page, and so on."

Getting the Most Out of Extended Writing Time

Cancel the share so there is more writing time, and rally kids to write fast and furious. Do this in ways that make a statement about the need to produce new writing often.

"Writers, we spent so much time helping each other and revising today that many of you haven't yet gotten very far in your new books. We wouldn't want today to go by without tons of writing, so let's work right past the share, to the very end of writing time. That gives you five more precious minutes for writing, so work fast as a bunny, and see how much you can get done in five minutes. Then, after five more minutes, we'll show each other how much we wrote today. You ready? On your mark, get set, go!"

As children wrote, I called out some voiceovers:

"Just because you are writing fast, you won't want to skip the details that really help people know what you mean."

"If you are writing just one sentence for each step, push yourself to say more, to add at least one more sentence to each step."

After children wrote, fast and furious, for five minutes, I said, "Wow! You all wrote so much! Show each other what you accomplished, and let's hear you complimenting each other. I should hear you saying things like, 'Great job. You really worked hard!'"

34

GRADE K: HOW-TO BOOKS

First 2 sups ✗ Go In
the Dog Bl !

Step 1: First 2 cups go in the dog bowl!

Fil the Athr
Bl with wotr

Step 2: Fill the other bowl with water.

Put the ~~wthr~~
~~Bl~~ Bls On the Matt

Step 3: Put the bowls on the mat.

Cal Hovr ovr
to Et

Step 4: Call her over to eat.

FIG. 4–2   Encourage children to make pictures that teach the most important information, as this student has done.

Writers Label Their Diagrams to Teach Even More Information

IN THIS SESSION, you'll teach students that writers add detailed information to their writing by labeling their diagrams.

GETTING READY

✔ Class shared writing on how to make a peanut butter and jelly sandwich with diagram added, covered with sheet of paper (see Teaching)

✔ Kids come to the carpet today with a marker or pen and a large Post-it stuck to a hard writing surface such as a clipboard or white board (see Active Engagement).

✔ "How-To Writing" anchor chart on display in the classroom (see Link)

✔ A volunteer in the class who will act as a teacher, using expressions, gestures, and pointing to teach the class how to follow the steps in his or her how-to book.

COMMON CORE STATE STANDARDS: W.K.2, W.K.5, RI.K.7, RFS.K.1.b; RFS.K.3.a,b; RFS.1.3.a,b,d,e; SL.K.1, SL.K.5, L.K.1, L.K.2.c,d; L.K.6

36

"WASSAT?" ASKS THE TODDLER, pointing at a tree.

"That's a tree," we say patiently.

"Wassat?" she asks, now pointing at the clouds. "Wassat?" Now pointing at the grandmother walking her dog. "Wassat? Wassat? Wassat?"

We all love a label. Even as we grow older, we look for language to pair with images. We may step in close to read the plate below a painting in a museum, looking for the artist's name, the date, and the title so that we can think more about what we see. Or we may part the leaves in a flat of annuals to read the little plastic spear, stuck into the dirt, that names the flower and tells us how much sun it needs and when to plant it. In books, we seek out the captions under photos, the labels on cross sections and graphs. No matter our age or experience, we all use labels to give shape and add meaning to images.

Today we invite children to help shape the meaning others take in when looking at the images they have created; we invite them to write labels.

In some ways this is a very basic session. The work seems supportive and uncomplicated. Once children have made an image, they need only point at some part of it and a word or phrase will come to their mind, and they will know what to write. On the other hand, this work is not as simple as it seems. To write a label very well, a person needs to think carefully about what the reader needs to know—and also what he doesn't need to know. Too much information is confusing!

Today's session, then, taps into our human need to put words to pictures, and yet it also nudges children to think about audience and to think about each detail's relative importance in a how-to text. These are not simple challenges, though every child will be able to find a successful way to handle them.

Our world is not a simple place with simple labels for things. This session is meant to move children farther along the path to learning that, while still setting them up to enjoy the concrete fun of drawing pictures and arrows and messing with sticky notes.

Writers Label Their Diagrams to Teach Even More Information

CONNECTION

Remind the class of the preceding day's problematic effort to follow your less-than-ideal directions, and point out that you learned you needed to add more detail.

"Remember the other day when the first draft of the peanut butter and jelly book said, 'Put the peanut butter on the bread?'" I acted this out again, with the jar balanced on the loaf. "That book didn't work at all, did it? I had to go back and write the book with more detail, so it said, 'Using a knife, scoop out a knife-sized lump of peanut butter.'

"What I learned from your help is that details really matter. Our book did a better job once we added details like 'open the peanut butter,' 'put the knife into it.' Right?"

❖ **Name the teaching point.**

"Today I want to teach you that one way that writers add detail to information books is by adding detailed pictures called *diagrams*. Writers often help readers understand their how-to books by making detailed diagrams and by labeling the diagrams, using the most precise, specific words they can."

TEACHING

Show that you have added detail to the preceding day's directions by adding a giant diagram, but without labels. Recruit children to join you in thinking about how this is different than illustrations in a picture book.

I unveiled an enlarged, poster-sized (not-yet-labeled) peanut butter and jelly diagram that I had intentionally kept under wraps until this moment. "Many of you have been asking me, 'What is under that sheet? What is it?'

"This is not just a regular picture of a peanut butter and jelly sandwich. With your partner, please think about how this is an unusual picture, and think about how this can help a writer to include details in her how-to book."

After the children discussed for a minute or two, I stopped the hubbub. "You are right that a diagram has much more detail than a regular picture. It shows all the parts and ingredients very clearly. This particular diagram is missing one thing that might add even more information. Thumbs up if you have an idea. Yes, you guessed it. Labels!"

During the connection component of a mini-lesson we often reiterate the content of the previous minilesson before teaching children the new focus of today's work.

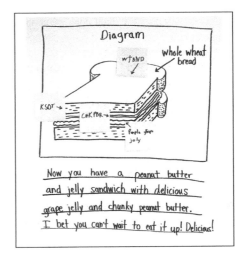

FIG. 5–1   Students and teacher collaborate to create a diagram for their shared writing.

It's fun to think up ways to make your lessons enticing. Whether you cover up the day's materials or put them in a box with a note saying, "Don't peek," you can find playful ways to encourage interest in the day's work.

SAMPLE BEND

37

Demonstrate how to label diagrams, using precise words.

"Watch how I label a few parts of my diagram as clearly and precisely as I can, using the most exact, specific words I can think of. I like to do it like this: first I point to a part. Then I try out saying a few different words and pick the clearest ones. Let's see this part there. That's the bread. The crust. Whole wheat bread, actually. That's it! I'll label it 'whole wheat bread.'" I stretched out the words and wrote them as I said this last part, just tucking in what kids already know about writing trickier words. I added an arrow pointing directly to the bread.

Restate what you've just done, naming each step explicitly.

"Did you see how I did that? First I pointed, then I said a few different words, and then I picked the best, most exact words I could think of to label one part of the diagram."

ACTIVE ENGAGEMENT

Recruit children to help you continue adding more labels to your diagram, prompting them to include specifics.

"All right, now it's your turn to give it a try! Each of you has a Post-it that you can use to make a label for our peanut butter and jelly diagram. Right now, if you are sitting on a red square or a green square, you can make a label for the top part of our class diagram. If you're sitting on a purple square or a blue square, you can make a label for the bottom part of the diagram. This way we will have labels for all the parts of the diagram. Remember, try to pick the very best, most precise words you can think of, words that will really help your reader understand what to do and how."

As I circulated around the carpet, I prompted a few kids to get more precise. "What kind of jelly was it, again?" "Was that crunchy peanut butter or smooth?" "How much jelly did we use? Oh, yeah, I think it was about a tablespoon." "Which label should your reader see first? I mean, which one should get the line all the way to the top of the page?"

As kids began to finish up, I collected a handful to show. "Writers, look up here. I think you guys are really getting the hang of adding lots of detailed, precise information to your diagrams. Check this out. Vivian wrote 'purple grape jelly' to use as a label right here, and Damien wrote 'chunky peanut butter' to use right here. I'm going to stick these labels on right here and here. I think the peanut butter one should go on the top, so the reader sees it first, and I think an arrow to the right place on the drawing will help too. That way it is *really* specific."

LINK

Before you send children off, remind them that as they revise, finish, or start new books, they can also provide detailed information by labeling their diagrams.

"You already know many ways to make sure your how-to books clearly teach readers how to do something. Remember our chart?" I pointed to the anchor chart that had been on display nearby the meeting area all week long.

It is helpful for young children to point to a part of the picture first and then label that part. The concreteness of touching the actual page makes it all the more explicit and engaging.

As you read this, you may notice that these labels aren't so much labels as they are phrases or captions. This is because we want to emphasize detail and writing information as much as possible in everything the children do in this unit—including the labels. Labeling with more specificity and detail will in turn lead to writing sentences with more detail and specificity.

38

GRADE K: HOW-TO BOOKS

50

Sample pages from Kindergarten, Unit 3, *How-To Books: Writing to Teach Others* — Bend I: "Writing How-To Books, Step by Step"

"Now I think we can add one more thing, can't we? Labels!" I added "has labels that teach" to the list.

"Today you might work on going back over all the books you have written to find places where you might add even clearer, more specific labels. Thumbs up if that's what you plan to do today." Almost every thumb went up. "You might also decide to finish a book you started yesterday. Thumbs up if you'll try that." Half of the kids kept their thumbs up. "It's great that some of you plan to do both of these things! You can use your writing time to do lots of different things—both go back to old pieces that you thought might be done and finish up ones you've just started. And, of course, you'll start new how-to books when you're ready. Remember, when you are writing how-to books, it often helps to label your diagrams with very clear and specific labels that teach the reader lots of information. You can write your labels straight into your book. You may want to use arrows and numbers to make sure your readers know what part of your diagram a label goes with.

"As you leave the meeting area and head to your writing spot, will you add your label to our class book?" I called each table to their writing spots, giving them time to stick their labels onto the peanut butter and jelly how-to book.

How-To Writing

1. Tells what to do, in steps.

2. Numbers the steps.

3. Has a picture for each step.

4. **Has labels that teach.**

FIG. 5–2   Diagrams with labels can be added as a separate page in a how-to book, or they may be incorporated into the steps, as this student has done.

For additional information and sample sessions, visit **www.UnitsofStudy.com**

51

Building Vocabulary and Developing Language

TODAY'S MINILESSON set your class up to be thinking carefully about word choice and vocabulary. It's likely that groups of children in your class will need your support in coming up with the precise, domain-specific words to label their diagrams. "How can my children write labels," you might ask, "if they simply don't know what all the parts are called?"

If you suspect this is the case with a particular child, you might decide to confer into vocabulary with her. Pull up next to her and ask her to say aloud the labels and sentences that will go with her picture. If she cannot, you could coach her by pointing to part of her picture and asking, "Is this a . . . ," naming the part of the object for her. When she says yes, ask her to say it back by simply asking, "What is this?" She'll then name the object for you. "Oh!" you'll say. "This is a . . . ," and you'll name the object again. "Try writing it!" Encourage the child to say the word herself slowly, stretching it out so she can really hear the sounds. "Write the sounds you hear." Of course, having an alphabet strip handy will be helpful.

By this point in the year, you know your children well. It's likely that you have identified a group of children who could benefit from more practice with oral rehearsal of their writing. Some children might say the steps of their own how-to books aloud in ways that sound choppy or disjointed, as though it must have been some other person who wrote the words. In a conference you might ask a child (or a small group of children) to "pretend to write" a page—to tell you aloud exactly what the page will say. The first time the child says a sentence aloud, it comes out choppy. They might be thinking of the words one at a time without putting the meaning of the whole sentence together. Ask them to say the sentence aloud to you again, perhaps with the same details that are included in the pictures, or perhaps with more smoothness. Let them know that saying it aloud again and again until it comes out how they want it is what writers do. Writers practice the way the words go until they like the flow. Ask them to rehearse the sentence even a third time, this time with expression. You might even model saying their sentence with the appropriate emphasis, and even gestures. "From now on," you might end, "try rehearsing your sentences three or four times before you write. That way you can really smooth out what you want to say. *Then*, try writing it."

MID-WORKSHOP TEACHING **Writers Use the Detailed Words in Their Diagrams to Write Sentences that Explain Their Steps**

"Writers, I am learning so much information just from your diagrams in your how-to books! Remember, all of the details in your pictures and labels can also help you to write your sentences. Let me show you what I mean.

"Take a look at our peanut butter and jelly how-to book. Notice all the great details we put into the picture and the labels. Would I just write, 'Look at the thing. Eat it.'? No, of course not! I want to try to use all the details in the picture when I write my sentences. I might write, 'Now you have a peanut butter and jelly sandwich with delicious grape jelly and chunky peanut butter. I bet you can't wait to eat it up! Delicious!' See how the second draft I just said uses the details from our labels?

"I'm going to add that now to our chart." I used a caret to insert the word *detailed* into step 1 on our anchor chart, so that students would be able to see it on the chart and remember this lesson. "Right now, try it. Point to something important in your diagram. Now make sure that you use that information when you write the steps on your page. Ready? Go ahead, get started."

How-To Writing

1. Tells what to do, in ^detailed^ steps.

2. Numbers the steps.

3. Has a picture for each step.

4. Has labels that teach.

40

GRADE K: HOW-TO BOOKS

52

Sample pages from Kindergarten, Unit 3, *How-To Books: Writing to Teach Others* — Bend I: "Writing How-To Books, Step by Step"

As Students Continue Working . . .

"I just saw Christian rereading the piece he just finished and starting a new book, just like that! Remember, after you've finished one book, reread and get started on a new one!"

"If you're not sure whether the labels you're adding to your diagrams are clear enough, just ask your writing partner or someone else sitting near you."

"Jarrett just told me about the diagram his mom and dad were studying last night when they were putting together the crib to get ready for his new brother or sister on the way. So cool! Diagrams with labels are everywhere—and they are so helpful, right Jarrett?"

SESSION 5: WRITERS LABEL THEIR DIAGRAMS TO TEACH EVEN MORE INFORMATION

41

Writers Read Their Writing with Expression

Recruit an expressive reader/writer to read the class his or her how-to text, complete with intonation and gestures.

"Readers, for the share today, I am going to step aside, and William is going to be your teacher!" During conferring time, I'd checked in with William to make sure he was up for this and to have him do a quick practice read. He was delighted! I continued, "But before I go anywhere, I just want you to notice some of the things that William does. I think you can do them, too." I ticked these points off on my fingers as I said them.

"William (one) raises his voice and slows down for the really important things. He also (two) uses hand gestures." I demonstrated the wagging finger, the mini hand-chop, and even the two-hands-over-his-head motion for the really exciting parts, without saying a word and stealing his thunder. "And he (three) points to the pictures that match what he is saying! William, will you come up here and teach us, from your book, how to ride a scooter?"

William came up to the front of the class. "First!" he exclaimed, holding one finger in the air. "You have to put on your helmet." He wagged his finger in the air and pointed to his picture. Then, with a mini-chopping motion for each word, he emphasized, "This. Is. Very. Important."

William continued on as the rest of the class listened, rapt.

"Wow! Guys, did you notice all the hand gestures? The expression? The pointing to pictures? Do you think you could be like William today when you teach your partner from your how-to book? Yes? Good. Turn to your partners now. Partner 2, it is your turn to go first!"

42

GRADE K: HOW-TO BOOKS

54   Sample pages from Kindergarten, Unit 3, *How-To Books: Writing to Teach Others* — Bend I: "Writing How-To Books, Step by Step"

Writers Write as Many Books as They Can

Dear Teachers,

Nothing is more consistently helpful for young writers than encouraging more writing. We all know that the more writers practice—with coaching—the more they will grow. That is why coaching your little ones to write more and more *and more* is crucial. Now is the time to focus on that point, since now children have a sense of the form in which they are writing. Now that they have already written several how-to books, they should begin to feel more secure in the genre, so encourage them to produce more books. With each new book, more of the process of writing in this form will become automatic, freeing up their minds for new learning.

You, too, probably have a strong sense by now of the form into which you are teaching. We offer a letter at this point rather than a more detailed description of the teaching we've done so that you have an opportunity, a little friendly nudge, to try your hand at writing (planning) more of your own teaching for this session. What follows are some suggestions for each of the structures of the session. Undoubtedly, you will have your own ideas and budding plans for ways to support children's writing stamina and ways to support them in writing more and more. These are simply our ideas to date for you to use as you see fit—as is all of the curriculum in these units.

MINILESSON

To rally children's attention for concentrating on increasing the volume of their writing, you might offer up a little analogy.

For example, you could tell children about when a friend taught you a dance called the Macarena. Your friend told you the steps to do, and you did one, then the next, slowly, deliberately, plodding your way through the process. And your friend said, "You got it! Now, do it faster, like this," and all of a sudden she was whirling through the dance steps in a way that left you saying, "Huh? What did you just do?"

COMMON CORE STATE STANDARDS: W.K.2, RFS.K.3.c; SL.K.1, L.K.1, L.K.2

So your friend showed you that, in fact, what she had done was just what you now knew how to do—slowly, step by step—but she was putting all the actions together in a way that just flowed along.

You could use that story to say, in your teaching point, that once they know all the steps to writing a how-to book, and they have slowly, carefully written a book or two, they need to learn to do all those steps much more quickly. The best way to learn that is to practice and to push themselves.

For the teaching portion of the minilesson, you need to decide what to teach and how to teach it. In a way, there is not much to teach if your message is just "Write more how-to books, and write them faster! Practice!" So this frees you to think about little tips you could give your students that will help them do just that. You might decide, for example, to teach your children a collection of tips that helps them develop the habit of writing faster, longer, and stronger. Those could include tips for writing with more flow. Writers benefit form saying a whole sentence at a time, then writing that sentence (and a period at the end) without stopping. That works better than saying a word, writing that word, taking a break, and then trying to think of the next word. Then, too, you could give tips for getting more writing done—such as setting a goal. The goal could be a number of lines per page or a number of pages per book or to finish a book in a day.

In addition to thinking about the content of the teaching part of your minilesson, you will want to think about the methods you will use during this portion of your minilesson, You have several methods of teaching to choose from. You could:

- **Demonstrate** a way of writing even more.

- **Set up an inquiry** by asking kids to figure out, with their partners, a way to write even more.

- **Explain** some ways that writers write even more, **and give an example** of someone who has done it.

If you've chosen to demonstrate in your teaching, you might say something like, "Children, one way writers manage to write more is by setting goals for themselves. I'm going to do that right now. Let me look over what I've written and give myself a goal. So far I've written about one line for each of my pages. I'm going to push myself, hmm, maybe double? Yes, I'm going to push myself to write two lines for each page from now on. It will be hard, but not too hard for me. I'm going to write two lines across the bottom of the pages in this new booklet to remind myself to fill them both up with writing, with more detail."

As usual in the active engagement, you'll ask children to try some of what you've demonstrated or described in the teaching portion of the minilesson. You might ask children to turn to their partner and talk over a goal they can give themselves that will help them write even more of their ideas. You might then ask them to plan a way to remind themselves of that goal, perhaps jotting a note or reminder of some kind on their next empty booklet or stack of booklets.

"Children," you might say, "writers are always thinking over ways to write more, to get more of their thinking on to the page, and oftentimes, writers figure out ways to set goals for themselves to help them write more. Throughout your lives, you can always pause to set a goal if you want to push yourself!" Then,

56

Sample pages from Kindergarten, Unit 3, *How-To Books: Writing to Teach Others* — Bend I: "Writing How-To Books, Step by Step"

as is often the case in the link portion of the minilesson, you might remind children of all the different kinds of work they can do today during the workshop, and of the resources in the room they can use to solve their own writing problems.

CONFERRING AND SMALL-GROUP WORK
Spelling Tricky Words as Best You Can and Moving On

Independent. Resourceful. Creative problem solvers. These are the words your want to be able to use when describing your kindergartners. Not quite there yet? There are a few common issues around independence that are helpful to hold in mind as you head off to confer—today, and every day.

First, it is imperative that children are able to maintain their work long enough for you to pull a student or a small group aside while the rest of the class continues writing on their own. Do you find that when you are working off to the side with just one or a few students, the rest of the class isn't getting very much done? If this is the case, then stamina needs to become your main focus for the whole class before you can resume individual conferring and small-group work. Try coaching the whole class with reminders such as, "Keep that pen in your hand the whole time, even when you are thinking! Don't stop!" or "When you finish one story, put it in your folder, and go straight to the writing center to get another booklet." You might decide to reemphasize drawing and labeling, or you might even introduce new writing utensils for the sheer purpose of enticing children to write. One simple trick is to switch from black pens to blue pens in the spring. Many teachers find that this small change is exciting enough to reinvigorate students. After trying a few of these strategies and reestablishing students' independence during writing time, you can begin to pull small groups and to confer one-on-one with students again.

With the whole class at work, there are bound to be some predictable issues that stump even the most resourceful of young writers. And one of those issues is, of course, spelling. Many of your children have probably begun to use letters and sounds and are beginning to build up a bank of words they know by sight. This means they also can begin to tell when a word is still not spelled correctly—even after they have labored over it, stretching out the sounds to hear them and recording the letters they hear. Some children will go back over the word again and again, reluctant to move on from that word because they know it doesn't look right. You may want to pull together a few children who fit this description to teach a strategy to help them give the word their best try, and most importantly, *move on*, even if the word isn't perfect. You might teach them the "give it a go" strategy: write the word three times on a Post-it to "give it a go" and then pick the one that looks best. A different strategy is to give the tricky word their best try and circle it if they know it still isn't perfect, so that they can ask their partner about it later or come back to it on another day. Whatever strategies you decide to teach, the most important thing is to emphasize that writers problem-solve, all the time, on their own. Independently. Resourcefully. Creatively.

SAMPLE BEND

MID-WORKSHOP TEACHING
Keep Your Pen in Your Hand the *Whole* Time!

You might be surprised to discover how many children are in the habit of writing one letter at a time, or only one word at a time, putting their pen down, and looking away from the page after each letter or word. Take a moment to observe your children's writing behaviors. Do they use an appropriate grip? Are they spending time tracing back over letters or words they already wrote? Are they forming letters by pulling down from the top? It's a wise idea to keep these behaviors in your mind, reminding children to practice strong habits that will lead to more writing.

For your mid-workshop teaching you might say, "Writers, I'm noticing that some of you are writing one letter at a time, putting your pen down in between each letter. You'll get a lot more writing done if you keep your pen in your hand the *whole* time. Try it now, everybody. Pick up your pen, like this." Then hold up your own pen, just like theirs. "Put your pen on the paper. Ready, set, start writing. And don't put that pen down." Watch as the children resume writing. If any kids put their pens down, say, "Everybody, even when you're thinking about what to write, think with your pen in your hand." Then you might move around the room using nonverbal gestures to remind kids not to put their pens down.

You might also remind writers of the saying they've heard before—"When you're done, you've just begun!"—to remind them to start a new piece as soon as they've finished.

SHARE

As you near the end of the first bend in the unit, you could use the share time to give children a sense of how well they are doing. You could build up excitement by letting kids know that tomorrow they'll have a very special writing workshop. They'll get to hang up one of their how-to books anywhere they want. You could take a few minutes today to show kids how to pick a piece to revise for your mini-publishing. As always, you will want to emphasize that writers choose pieces that they really love to revise and publish. "Right now, could all of you look in your writing folder to pick out just one special how-to book? Pick one that you would like to work on even more. We will have time tomorrow to revise these and make them even better." You might have kids mark their chosen piece with a special star-shaped Post-it or a special sticker, so that tomorrow, they'll already have one piece picked out.

Perhaps you'll take the share time today to pose a question to the kids. "Where could we display our how-to books in this room?" Invite the kids to look around the room for places that might make sense, and perhaps you'll make a few suggestions to get the ideas flowing. "What about 'How to Wash Your Hands' next to the sink?" you might say, knowing full well that one of your students has written that very how-to book. "What about a basket of how-to books in our classroom library? How many of you might want to put one of your how-to books in there? Or what about hanging some on our class writing bulletin board?"

Enjoy!

Lucy, Beth, and Laurie

46

GRADE K: HOW-TO BOOKS

58   Sample pages from Kindergarten, Unit 3, *How-To Books: Writing to Teach Others* — Bend I: "Writing How-To Books, Step by Step"

Writers Reflect and Set Goals to Create Their Best Information Writing

THE SIMPLE ACT of noticing and naming the work that each child has done pays off in a number of important ways. Doing this makes the work more memorable and replicable and gives children vocabulary for talking and thinking about their own writing. That is why teaching children to look back over their own writing again and again is crucial. Periodically, in any unit, you will want to take time for kids to reread the work in their writing folders, pointing to, naming, and talking about the texts they have written so far—and to make plans for those they intend to write in the near future.

By now your children have written many how-to books, and they have had plenty of practice with several of the key features of the genre. With each new book, the process is becoming more automatic, and the quality of the writing is elevated.

As mentioned in earlier sessions, the Common Core State Standards offer a vision for what kindergarten informational writing can be. According to the standards, kindergartners will "use a combination of drawing, dictating, and writing to compose informative/explanatory texts in which they name what they are writing about and supply some information about the topic." This works with how-to book writing as well as it does with other types of informational writing. How will your children know if they are approaching this goal as they write how-to books?

In this lesson, you will help the children pause to reflect on the work they've done so far. To help children concretely understand the concept of reflection, we suggest showing them two examples of one student's work that clearly illustrate how that student's writing has grown over time. In this session we compare the how-to book of a child who is now in first grade to a how-to book he wrote in kindergarten. You could just as easily use one of your own student's pieces of writing from September to compare to the work the child is doing now or even create two contrasting examples of writing yourself. In any case, your goal in this lesson is to highlight that writers grow—a lot. And they grow because they set goals for themselves and they work hard to get there.

In this lesson, the children use star stickers to mark the spots in their writing where they are already meeting the expectations. The power is not in the stickers, of course, but

IN THIS SESSION, you'll teach students that writers draw on all they have learned about information writing, and they use an information writing checklist to set writing goals.

GETTING READY

✔ Student writing folders (see Connection)

✔ Information Writing Checklist, Grades K and 1 (see Connection)

✔ Enlarged copies of two pieces of student work from a former student (if possible), one from kindergarten and one from first grade. Student work from a current student could be substituted here (see Teaching).

✔ A strip of eight gold star stickers for each student as well as some for you to demonstrate with. Colored pen, marker, other labels, or stickers could be substituted (See Active Engagement).

✔ Personal copies of the Information Writing Checklist for kids (see Active Engagement)

COMMON CORE STATE STANDARDS: W.K.2, W.K.5, W.1.2, RI.K.1, RFS.K.1.b; RFS.K.3, RFS.1.3, SL.K.1, SL.K.2, SL.K.3, L.K.1, L.K.2.c,d; L.K.6

SAMPLE BEND

in the idea that we can concretely mark places in our writing that illustrate certain qualities. If you prefer, instead of stickers, you could give children special colored pens and invite them to underline or circle or star particular places in pieces of writing that show that they have tried each of the elements of strong informational writing.

"The simple act of noticing and naming the work that each child has done makes the work more memorable and replicable and gives children vocabulary for talking and thinking about their own writing."

This lesson is unusual in that you will be guiding children step by step to notice each of the items on the Information Writing Checklist from Unit 1. Usually in minilessons, you show a quick example and then send writers off to work on their own.

Of course, there will be items on the list that some children have not yet incorporated into their independent work. This is actually the most important part of the lesson: helping children to identify and record these goals. One way to

help children keep track of their goals is to give each child a mini version of the Information Writing Checklist so that they might point to, or even mark, the items on the list they want to keep working on. Given kindergartners' love of stickers, you might say, for example, "If you can't find a place in your writing where you wrote words to tell about your pictures, you can put a star sticker on your mini chart to remind you to keep working on that! You can keep it in your writing folder to remind you of the things you want to keep working on every day as a writer."

You may decide to go one step further and use homemade labels with icons for each item on the list. You might use a heart for "I told what my topic was," or an easel or chalkboard for "I put different things I know about the topic on my page," or an exclamation point for "I told, drew, and wrote some important things about the topic." As you coach students to find the places in their writing where they have done these things, you can observe to see who in your class places a label even thought they haven't yet accomplished the goal. This is a teachable moment.

Being explicit is incredibly helpful and important. You will want to make it known that the items on the list are indeed the goals of the unit and that the ultimate goal would be to find *all* of the items in *every* piece of writing. The link in today's lesson is a message to the children as well as a reminder to you: "Now that you've reflected on all the work you've accomplished so far, decide on some of the things you need to keep working on. We still have plenty of time in this unit for everybody to get all of these into all their writing. Let's get started now!"

Writers Reflect and Set Goals to Create Their Best Information Writing

CONNECTION

Remind students that writers hold onto and use things they've already learned.

"Writers, bring your folders and come to the meeting area," I said, and once the children were gathered on the carpet, I began. "Do you remember last month, when we were writing true stories, I reminded you that even when you are learning many new things, you also need to remember that you *already know how* to do many things? Remember that? We looked at our old charts and used them to help us remember to do everything that we already knew *and* to do all the new things too. This is an important thing to do no matter what kind of writing you're doing. We can do it with our how-to books, too!

"When I was going through old charts, not only did I find the old 'How to Write a True Story' chart, but I also found the Information Writing Checklist. Do you remember when we made this way back at the beginning of the year?" (See p. 53; the full-size Information Writing Checklist can be found on the CD-ROM.)

Briefly review the old chart with your students to make sure it's fresh in their minds, keeping in mind that you will be going through the list again in detail shortly.

"Right now, let's read this chart together and try to remember when we first learned to do all of these important things."

I quickly read each item on the chart aloud, pausing for children to have a chance to think back, saying "Thumbs up if you remember way back in September when we first learned this."

Name the teaching point.

"Today I want to teach you that even though you are learning all these important new things about how-to books, you still need to remember everything you already learned about writing informational books. You can use old charts to help you keep track of all the work you are already doing and to help you set new goals."

♦ COACHING

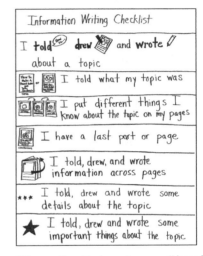

FIG. 7–1 Your kindergarteners will benefit from picture support added to the Information Writing Checklist. This chart can remain on display throughout the remainder of the unit as a tool for checking in on goals for information writing. The chart used in this session does not include the Conventions section of the complete checklist, because conventions will be highlighted later in the unit.

This is essentially the same teaching point you taught early in the Writing for Readers *unit. Strong teaching often revisits strategies again and again in new contexts.*

49

SAMPLE BEND

TEACHING

Using two pieces of student writing that illustrate growth over time, highlight the idea that writers grow when they set goals and work toward them.

"This morning when I was walking down the hall to our classroom, one of my old students who is in first grade now, Luke, came running up to me. Some of you know him, don't you? Well, Luke was all excited because his class had just finished writing all-about books, and he couldn't wait to show me. He took me over to his class's bulletin board in the hallway, and I read his writing, and you know what? It was a-ma-zing how much Luke had grown as a writer, and he told me it was because he was always setting goals for himself and had worked really, really hard to reach them. I was so proud of him. In fact, when I got to our room this morning I looked through my old files and I found an old, old piece of Luke's writing from last year, and I asked him if I could share it with you guys, so you could see how much you can grow from kindergarten to first grade."

I had taped a photocopy of Luke's kindergarten writing on chart paper, above a photocopy of his latest first-grade writing. The difference was obvious.

Step 1: First take the connector and plug it in next . . . Be careful. Do not push too hard.

Step 2: Open the DVD holder next . . . Do not put your finger in the DVD holder.

Step 3: Put the DVD in next . . .

Step 4: Turn on the TV next . . .

Step 5: You play Play Station 2.

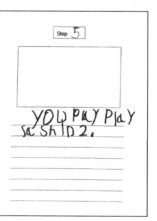

FIG. 7–2 Luke's piece from kindergarten

50

Positions

In football there is a lot of positions in football. One position is a quarterback. A quarterback's job is to throw the ball and run the ball and snap the ball. The kicker kicks the ball for a field goal or return the ball.

Gear

In football you need gear. A type of gear is football pants. Another type of gear is a helmet. Another is shoulder pads. Another is a cup. Another is cleats. Oh, and wait. I meant a football cup, not a real cup.

Equipment

In football you need equipment. One type of equipment is a football. Another is a field goal. Another is a field.

Team

In football there are teams. One team is the Texas Longhorns. Another is the New England Patriots. Another is the Jets. Another is the Giants. Another is the Baltimore Ravens. Another is the Dallas Cowboys.

Closing

Now you know all about football. See you on the field. Do not forget your cup.

FIG. 7–3   Luke's piece from first grade

SESSION 7: WRITERS REFLECT AND SET GOALS TO CREATE THEIR BEST INFORMATION WRITING   51

After the giggling had subsided (yes, Luke's piece was funny), I continued. "Wow. What do you guys notice? Turn and tell your partner." I listened in as partners began to talk.

"I know! It's really incredible isn't it? How many of you noticed that Luke used to write just a little bit on each page, but now you can see that he really says a lot of information for every page?" Nearly all of the kids' hands flew up. "You know what? I'm going to put a little note here for Luke, a little star sticker to let him know that we noticed that he's really writing a lot of information on each page. Don't you think he would like that?"

I peeled off a star sticker and stuck it right on a particularly detailed portion of the drawing.

Suggest that students use the Information Writing Checklist to determine which writing goals they have met and which they can work toward, making note of each in a concrete way.

"I noticed that some of you weren't sure what to look for in Luke's writing. Hey, couldn't we use our Information Writing Checklist to look at Luke's writing? Let's try that together. I'll go down the checklist, and you guys go like this with your hands to show me if we could give Luke a star for it." I made a star gesture by bunching my hand in a fist, and then spreading it out again, like a shooting star. "Why don't you all give it a try now?"

Referring to the checklist and Luke's older piece of writing, I asked, "How many of you noticed that Luke put different things he knows about a topic across the pages? Don't say anything. Just remember our star sign!" The kids unanimously gave him the star gesture, something that I now (happily) realized was going to live in our classroom for quite a while. I peeled off another star and stuck it on his writing. The kids were rapt. It was obvious to me now that the whole class was wondering, "Are we going to get to use stickers?"

I pointed out that Luke had also made a final page for his how-to, to let us know when all the steps were done, the fourth item on our checklist. Another star. I moved on to the next item on the list, "I told, drew, and wrote information across the pages." I stopped. "Huh. I'm not so sure about this one. He has a lot of information in his words, but there are no pictures! There is a lot more he could have shown. What should I do?" The kids looked a little concerned. I could tell what they were thinking, "No star? But we like giving stars!"

"Hey, I know what we could do!" I pulled out a smaller version of the Information Writing Checklist that I had already prepared. "We could give him a copy of our chart, like this, to let him know some things he could keep working on—so he can reach for more stars!" I read the line on the card, "I told, drew, and wrote about a topic," and stuck a star next to it. "What do you guys think about that?" "Yes!" the kids shouted.

ACTIVE ENGAGEMENT

Tell students they will be noting goals accomplished and goals to work toward.

"So, writers, how would you like to give yourselves some stars to show what goals you've accomplished and which ones you're working toward? Right now, I'm going to give each of you some special star stickers and your own copy

When you introduce the Information Writing Checklist to your class, you might want to begin with the items that are most familiar, or that lend themselves to the particular piece of writing you are using. I decided not to begin at the top of the list, because I knew that it would be easier for children to recognize that yes, Luke did put different things that he knows.

Telling, drawing, and writing are all included in the Information Writing Checklist because all three are important expectations for kindergarteners to demonstrate in their work. You might discover that children in your class are leaning heavily on one or the other, instead of utilizing all three. When a child or group of children (or whole class) needs extra support in any one of the three, then that becomes a goal to teach into in a conference, small group, or minilesson.

of the Information Writing Checklist that you can use to keep track of the goals you're still working toward. We're going to go down the checklist together to see which items on the list are goals you've met (you'll put stars right in your books where you notice those goals) and which items on the list are goals you're still working toward. You'll stick those stars on your own copy of the Information Writing Checklist."

I passed a strip of eight stars to each student (one star for each item on the checklist, plus one extra), plus small copies of the Kindergarten and First Grade Information Writing Checklists that I had already prepared.

Guide the children through the checklist step by step, showing them how to mark their how-to books where they have accomplished a goal and how to mark their card when they are still working toward a goal.

"Let's begin with 'I told, drew, and wrote about a topic.' Right now, look through your folder and choose a piece that shows you did this." I paused while children selected a piece of writing. "Let's make sure. Thumbs up if you can *tell* out loud the information in your how-to. Great. Thumbs up if you *drew* pictures that teach the steps on

Information Writing Checklist

	Kindergarten	NOT YET	STARTING TO	YES!	Grade 1	NOT YET	STARTING TO	YES!
	Structure				**Structure**			
Overall	I told, drew, and wrote about a topic.	☐	☐	☐	I taught my readers about a topic.	☐	☐	☐
Lead	I told what my topic was.	☐	☐	☐	I named my topic in the beginning and got my readers' attention.	☐	☐	☐
Transitions	I put different things I knew about the topic on my pages.	☐	☐	☐	I told different parts about my topic on different pages.	☐	☐	☐
Ending	I had a last part or page.	☐	☐	☐	I wrote an ending.	☐	☐	☐
Organization	I told, drew, and wrote information across pages.	☐	☐	☐	I told about my topic part by part.	☐	☐	☐
	Development				**Development**			
Elaboration	I drew and wrote important things about the topic.	☐	☐	☐	I put facts in my writing to teach about my topic.	☐	☐	☐
Craft	I told, drew, and wrote some details about the topic.	☐	☐	☐	I used labels and words to give facts.	☐	☐	☐
	Language Conventions				**Language Conventions**			
Spelling	I could read my writing.	☐	☐	☐	I used all I knew about words and chunks (*at, op, it,* etc.) to help me spell.	☐	☐	☐
	I wrote a letter for the sounds I heard.	☐	☐	☐	I spelled the word wall words right and used the word wall to help me spell other words.	☐	☐	☐
	I used the word wall to help me spell.	☐	☐	☐				

all your pages. Nice. Okay, now thumbs up if you also *wrote* the steps on each page. Excellent. If you gave yourself a thumbs-up for all of these, stick a star on that piece of writing! If you didn't draw all your pictures or if you didn't write words yet—just stick the star right onto your mini-copy of our Information Writing Checklist to remind yourself to work on it." I pointed to the bigger copy of the checklist to show them where that star would go.

I continued on to the next item on the checklist in the same fashion, and the next, sometimes moving around to coach children who seemed puzzled, occasionally suggesting to particular children that they mark their checklist instead of just putting the star anywhere. I knew that over time, the checklist would become very familiar to kids, as I planned on using it often in conferences and small groups to help kids figure out what to work on.

"Writers, I am so proud of all of you. Look at how much you already know how to do as writers. There is just one last thing. Remember I said I was going to teach you to use the chart to keep track of all that you are doing *and* to help you set goals? Lots of you already marked your checklist with one or two things to work on. Now everyone should have one last sticker left. Right now, if you haven't marked anything on your checklist yet, either pick one thing to reach for, or you could even write something on your list. You could put a question mark there if you aren't sure what to work on, or you could pick something from our other charts to work on."

As children move through the grades, the work they do each year will stand on the shoulders of years' past. For today's session, you might adapt the kindergarten and first-grade checklist to contain as many or as few items as needed. You might also use the first-grade checklist as an alternative if it is a better fit for the characteristics of your young writers. Try to avoid using a checklist where children will simply check off everything as "done." On the other hand, you won't want a checklist where the children have nothing at all to check off.

SESSION 7: WRITERS REFLECT AND SET GOALS TO CREATE THEIR BEST INFORMATION WRITING

53

LINK

Before sending them off to work, ask students to use the Information Writing Checklist to tell their writing partners what they plan to work on.

"Writers, this year all of you are going to grow as writers just as much as Luke did. And it all starts right now. Last year, Luke was just like you, and he kept setting goals and working on them, just like you did today. You've just given yourself stars for all the great things you already know how to do, and you also have a few things to reach for. Right now, turn to the person next to you and use the stars that you placed on your checklist to tell them what you are going to work on today, and every day, in your writing."

If you find that reflecting on every item on the checklist is going to take too long, you might do part of the checklist in the minilesson, and the rest of the checklist during a mid-workshop teaching point, or the share.

Information Writing Checklist Scully

I told drew and wrote about a topic

I told what my topic was

I put different things I know about the topic on my pages

I have a last part or page

I told, drew, and wrote information across pages

★ ★ ★ I told, drew and wrote some details about the topic

★ I told, drew and wrote some important things about the topic

54

GRADE K: HOW-TO BOOKS

66

Sample pages from Kindergarten, Unit 3, *How-To Books: Writing to Teach Others* — Bend I: "Writing How-To Books, Step by Step"

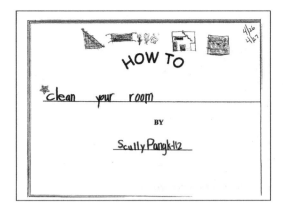

HOW TO

*clean your room

BY

Scully Pangk-ll2

First you goto your room.

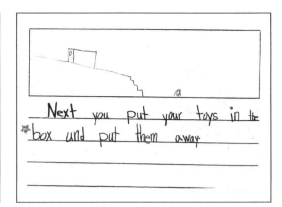

_Next you put your toys in the *box and put them away

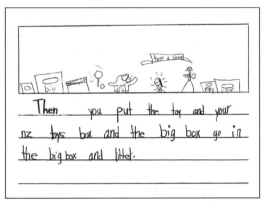

Then you put the toy and your nz toys box and the big box go in the big box and littel.

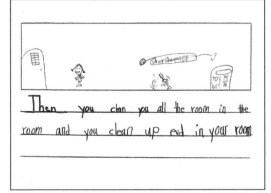

Then you chan you all the room in the room and you clean up evd in your room

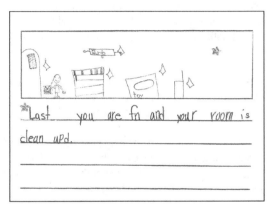

*Last you are fn and your room is clean upd.

FIG 7–4   With the help of a teacher, Scully decides that his writing could use more detail. Future lessons on elaboration and using detail in the pictures to fuel more writing will help Scully become a more detailed writer.

SAMPLE BEND

Helping Writers Keep Everything They've Learned in Mind as They Work

I HAD CONFERRED WITH JONATHAN at the beginning of work time about adding more details to his drawings so that readers would really be able to picture the steps of his how-to book about making a Lego space ship. His drawings had been so spare it was hard to see a difference between steps. Knowing that Jonathan's drawing skill had increased dramatically since the beginning of the year when he was not yet drawing representationally, I pushed for more detail and clarity in his how-to book drawings. He was game and immediately started adding details.

After conferring with a couple more students, I circled back around to check on Jonathan and discovered that he was still on the same page of his how-to book! That page was packed with details. But that was all he had done since I'd seen him last.

Whenever we introduce something new, sometimes children focus on that one thing to the exclusion of everything else they've learned. This is completely normal. The pendulum swings hard in the direction of the new learning. It can take some time—and some reminders from you—to bring back the balance.

I knelt down by Jonathan and said, "Wow, Jonathan, you sure have been working hard on adding details to your pictures. Your readers have so much more information now! It will be a lot easier for them to understand how to make this ship. Jonathan beamed.

"Can I see what you've worked on on the other pages of your book?" I asked this knowing that Jonathan had not, in fact, even turned the page, but the question implied that there was other work to be done.

"I just was adding details to here," he said. "See the number? It's spaceship 5!"

"This is so great, Jonathan," I said. "You really are helping your readers by adding more details to that picture. But here's the thing. I know I reminded you that writers add important details to their pictures today, but that doesn't mean that adding details is the *only* work you do today. Right? Writers have so many things to keep in mind, and

MID-WORKSHOP TEACHING
Writers Want Feedback on Their Hard Work

"Writers, eyes up here for a moment, please. When writers work very hard and have tried to make their writing the best they've ever written, they want to get feedback on their work. They want to hear what they've done well, but they also want to hear things that can make their books even better. Using your best teaching voice, will Partner 1 read the how-to book that you think is your best to Partner 2? Then, partners, please give feedback. Don't just say, 'I like your book.' Say, 'I like your how-to book because I was able to follow your directions,' or 'I like your how-to book because I could read it clearly.'"

sometimes when you are working on one thing, you can forget about all of the other things we've been learning about and practicing."

This elicited a large sigh from Jonathan. "Don't be discouraged! You're doing such grown-up work. You really focused on trying out adding more details. That's huge! But I want to remind you that writers also keep in mind all the other things they know. What else have we been working on that you could think about as you finish your book?"

"It's gotta make sense," he offered.

"So true!" I said. "Maybe you could read through it and see if the steps make sense and if your words have as many details as your pictures. But that's just one idea. I want to remind you that when writers are working, they keep in mind not just *one* thing they've learned, but *all* of the things they've been learning."

Jonathan flipped back to the beginning of his book and started rereading.

56

Getting How-To Books into Readers' Hands

To create a mini-celebration, suggest that writers distribute their how-to books to appropriate places around the room and the school.

"Writers, I know we usually don't put our writing out on shelves for people to read until the end of the unit, but some of your how-to books could be useful to this class right now. Remember yesterday when I mentioned that we'd be putting some of your how-to books out so that people could actually start using them? Like this book about how to clean a hamster cage. I don't think we should wait to put it into a place where people will find it when they need it. A book on how to jump on a trampoline could go in the how-to book basket we made for our classroom library or maybe on the how-to book bulletin board in the hall. I'm thinking that first you'll need to choose two of your how-to books, books that you think people will be able to start using right away, and then work together to figure out where you can put them in the school so that they'll be really useful. Are you game?"

Of course they were! As children spoke with their writing partners about where they wanted to put their how-to books, I started taping some of the how-to books to their chosen spots. As children saw me do this, they were inspired to think of new places to put how-to books, and soon there were books everywhere. "How to Wash Your Hands" was hanging right by the sink in the classroom. "How to Do a Fire Drill" went by the door (see Figure 7–5 on next page). "How to Shop for Books" was placed right by the classroom library, and "How to Be Principal for the Day" was on its way to being hung on the door in the principal's office.

SAMPLE BEND

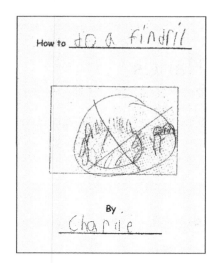
How to do a findrill

By: Charlie

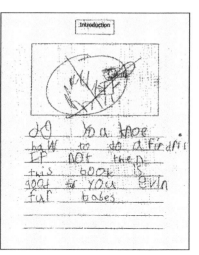
do Yo a tnoe
haW to do a findrie
IF NOt then
this book is
good for you evin
fur babes

Things You Need...
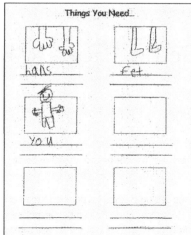
hans   fet

you

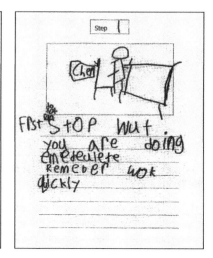
FRst StOP wut
you are doing
emedeulete
remeber wok
quickly

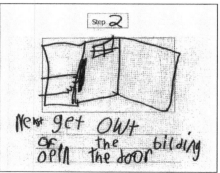
Next get OWt
of the bilding
opEn the door

Next wat 5 minits
and then go
bakin

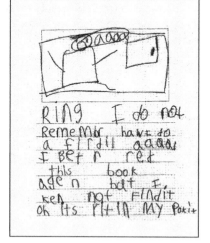
RING I do not
rememr haw to
a fErdil gaaa
I Bet n red
this book
agen bat I
ken not FINdit
oh its rt in MY Poki+

Wok in the
door

Then You ken
go bat to
wat You wrdoing

FIG. 7–5   Charlie's Fire Drill How-To book

58

Writing Pathways is designed to help you provide your students with continuous assessment, feedback, and goal setting. Organized around a K–5 continuum of **learning progressions** for opinion, information, and narrative writing, this practical guide includes **performance assessments, learning progressions, student checklists, rubrics,** and **leveled writing exemplars** that help you evaluate your students' work and establish where students are in their writing development.

❞ The assessment system that undergirds this curriculum is meant as an instructional tool. It makes progress in writing as transparent, concrete, and obtainable as possible and puts ownership for this progress into the hands of learners. This system of assessment demystifies the Common Core State Standards, allowing students and teachers to work toward a very clear image of what good work entails. ❞

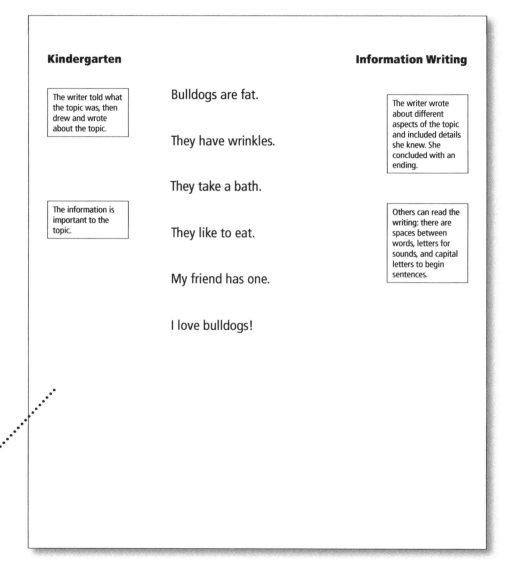

Kindergarten   **Information Writing**

The writer told what the topic was, then drew and wrote about the topic.

Bulldogs are fat.

They have wrinkles.

The writer wrote about different aspects of the topic and included details she knew. She concluded with an ending.

They take a bath.

The information is important to the topic.

They like to eat.

Others can read the writing: there are spaces between words, letters for sounds, and capital letters to begin sentences.

My friend has one.

I love bulldogs!

An exemplar piece of writing for each writing genre shows how one piece of writing could develop according to the learning progressions established by the Common Core State Standards.

The units teach students the CCSS' grade-appropriate skills for both their own grade level and for the upcoming grade. That is, the kindergarten information writing unit supports both the kindergarten and the first-grade standards. This is done in part because the expectation level of the CCSS for middle school is exceedingly high. For an entire class of students to reach the sixth- and eighth-grade CCSS expectations when they reach those grade levels, teachers need to accelerate students' writing development in the early grades, when the Common Core Standards in writing do not keep the same fast pace as the reading standards.

Crystal-clear checklists that spell out the genre-specific benchmarks students should be working toward help students set goals and self-assess their work.

Information Writing Checklist (continued)

	Kindergarten	NOT YET	STARTING TO	YES!	Grade 1	NOT YET	STARTING TO	YES!
Punctuation	I put spaces between words.	☐	☐	☐	I ended sentences with punctuation.	☐	☐	☐
	I used lowercase letters unless capitals were needed.	☐	☐	☐	I used a capital letter for names.	☐	☐	☐
	I wrote capital letters to start every sentence.	☐	☐	☐	I used commas in dates and lists.	☐	☐	☐

Name: _____ Date: _____

Information Writing Checklist

	Kindergarten	NOT YET	STARTING TO	YES!	Grade 1	NOT YET	STARTING TO	YES!
	Structure				**Structure**			
Overall	I told, drew, and wrote about a topic.	☐	☐	☐	I taught my readers about a topic.	☐	☐	☐
Lead	I told what my topic was.	☐	☐	☐	I named my topic in the beginning and got my readers' attention.	☐	☐	☐
Transitions	I put different things I knew about the topic on my pages.	☐	☐	☐	I told different parts about my topic on different pages.	☐	☐	☐
Ending	I had a last part or page.	☐	☐	☐	I wrote an ending.	☐	☐	☐
Organization	I told, drew, and wrote information across pages.	☐	☐	☐	I told about my topic part by part.	☐	☐	☐
	Development				**Development**			
Elaboration	I drew and wrote important things about the topic.	☐	☐	☐	I put facts in my writing to teach about my topic.	☐	☐	☐
Craft	I told, drew, and wrote some details about the topic.	☐	☐	☐	I used labels and words to give facts.	☐	☐	☐
	Language Conventions				**Language Conventions**			
Spelling	I could read my writing.	☐	☐	☐	I used all I knew about words and chunks (*at, op, it,* etc.) to help me spell.	☐	☐	☐
	I wrote a letter for the sounds I heard.	☐	☐	☐	I spelled the word wall words right and used the word wall to help me spell other words.	☐	☐	☐
	I used the word wall to help me spell.	☐	☐	☐				

WRITING PATHWAYS, K–5

Rubrics for each kind of writing establish clear benchmarks that help teachers monitor student progress.

Name: _____ Date: _____

Rubric for Information Writing—Kindergarten

	Pre-Kindergarten (2 POINTS)	2.5 PTS	Kindergarten (3 POINTS)	3.5 PTS	Grade 1 (4 POINTS)	SCORE
STRUCTURE						
Overall	The writer told and drew pictures about a topic she knew.	Mid-level	The writer told, drew, and wrote about a topic.	Mid-level	The writer taught readers about a topic.	
Lead	The writer started by drawing or saying something.	Mid-level	The writer told what her topic was.	Mid-level	The writer named his topic in the beginning and got the readers' attention.	
Transitions	The writer kept on working.	Mid-level	The writer put different things he knew about the topic on his pages.	Mid-level	The writer told different parts about her topic on different pages.	
Ending	After the writer said, drew, and "wrote" all he could about his topic, he ended it.	Mid-level	The writer had a last part or page.	Mid-level	The writer wrote an ending.	
Organization	On the writer's paper, there was a place for the drawing and a place where she tried to write words.	Mid-level	The writer told, drew, and wrote information across pages.	Mid-level	The writer told about her topic part by part.	
						TOTAL
DEVELOPMENT						
Elaboration*	The writer put more and then more on the page.	Mid-level	The writer drew and wrote some important things about the topic.	Mid-level	The writer put facts in his writing to teach about his topic.	(X2)
Craft*	The writer said, drew, and "wrote" things she knew about the topic.	Mid-level	The writer told, drew, and wrote some details about the topic.	Mid-level	The writer used labels and words to give facts.	(X2)
						TOTAL

* Elaboration and Craft are double-weighted categories: Whatever score a student would get in these categories is worth double the amount of points. For example, if a student exceeds expectations in Elaboration, then that student would receive 8 points instead of 4 points. If a student meets standards in Elaboration, then that student would receive 6 points instead of 3 points.

	Pre-Kindergarten (2 POINTS)	2.5 PTS	Kindergarten (3 POINTS)	3.5 PTS	Grade 1 (4 POINTS)	SCORE
LANGUAGE CONVENTIONS						
Spelling	The writer could read his pictures and some of his words. The writer tried to make words.	Mid-level	The writer could read her writing. The writer wrote a letter for the sounds she heard. The writer used the word wall to help her spell.	Mid-level	The writer used all he knew about words and chunks (*at*, *op*, *it*, etc.) to help him spell. The writer spelled the word wall words right and used the word wall to help him spell other words.	
Punctuation	The writer could label pictures. The writer could write her name.	Mid-level	The writer wrote spaces between words. The writer used lowercase letters unless capitals were needed. The writer wrote capital letters to start every sentence.	Mid-level	The writer ended sentences with punctuation. The writer used a capital letter for names. The writer used commas in dates and lists.	
						TOTAL

Teachers, we created these rubrics so you will have your own place to pull together scores of student work. You can use these assessments immediately after giving the on-demands and also for self-assessment and setting goals.

Scoring Guide

In each row, circle the descriptor in the column that matches the student work. Scores in the categories of Elaboration and Craft are worth double the point value (*4, 5, 6, 7,* or *8* instead of *2, 2.5, 3, 3.5,* or *4*).

Total the number of points and then track students' progress by seeing when the total points increase.

Total score: _____

If you want to translate this score into a grade, you can use the provided table to score each student on a scale of 0–4.

Number of Points	Scaled Score
2–22	2
22.5–27.5	2.5
28–33	3
33.5–38.5	3.5
39–44	4

In addition to the four units of study, the Kindergarten series provides a book of if... then... curricular plans. ***If... Then... Curriculum: Assessment-Based Instruction, Kindergarten*** supports targeted instruction and differentiation with six alternative units of study for you to strategically teach before, after, or in between the core curriculum based on your students' needs. This resource also includes If... Then... Conferring Scenarios that help you customize your curriculum through individual and small-group instruction.

"The quality of writing instruction will rise dramatically not only when teachers study the teaching of writing but also when teachers study their own children's intentions and progress as writers. Strong writing is always tailored for and responsive to the writer."

ALTERNATE UNIT

**Storytelling across the Pages:
First Steps for Personal Narrative Writing**

IF your students are still not writing simple sequenced narratives by the end of the *Launching the Writing Workshop* unit OR your students are writing letters or words on the page without any meaning or story to go with them, THEN you might want to teach this unit before *Writing for Readers*.

Storytelling across the Pages
First Steps for Personal Narrative Writing

RATIONALE/INTRODUCTION

This unit will invite kindergartners to embark on work that will surely dazzle you and the kids. Expect the unit to be a smash hit! In this unit you will explicitly teach students to tell organized, structured stories that proceed chronologically through the sequence of a small event. If you have the video *Big Lessons from Small Writers* (and we urge you to get it if you do not), you'll want to watch the young writers work on their true stories—especially Harold, who writes, "I woke up. I put on my pants, I put on my shoes. Then I walked to school." That's the work of this unit.

This unit is a sort of precursor to the work children will do in the *Writing for Readers* unit. In that book, Lucy Calkins and Natalie Louis show you how children can begin to write stories that others can read, writing meaningful moments from their very own lives and using all that they know about spelling and conventions to make their writing easy for others to read. All of this work is in line with the Common Core State Standards, which channel kindergartners to produce narrative stories through a combination of drawing and writing and add to do this in such a way that they narrate a single event or several loosely linked events. You might also look to the Rubric for Narrative Writing, available on the CD-ROM, to set goals for their narrative writing across the year.

Some goals of the unit, then, are for your youngsters to generate true stories from their lives, recording these stories across the pages of little booklets using representational drawings. You'll want them to tell cohesive, sequenced narratives, and label many items on each page. You'll want children to be able to "reread" the books they write, turning the pages from front to back, "reading" them from left to right, top to bottom. They will work in partnerships, sharing their booklets. You'll want them to tell their stories using rich, oral storytelling language. They can sit hip-to-hip, hold the booklet between them, turn pages (ideally from left to right), and tell the story as they study the pictures and "read" the writing. They can begin working on one-to-one matches as they name the things that they see on the page and read the labels under each of those items.

2

IF...THEN...CURRICULUM, KINDERGARTEN

76   UNITS OF STUDY IN OPINION, INFORMATION, AND NARRATIVE WRITING • *If... Then... Curriculum: Assessment-Based Instruction, Kindergarten*

ALTERNATE UNIT
Writing All-About Books

IF you want to give your students an opportunity to write expository informational texts about their own areas of personal expertise, THEN you may want to teach this unit. It builds on the work of *How-To Books: Writing to Teach Others*.

Writing All-About Books

RATIONALE/INTRODUCTION

Let's face it: your class is teeming with youngsters full of passions and areas of expertise. The child who knows everything about dolphins, the child who can tell you twelve million facts about makeup, the snake enthusiast, or the aspiring engineer who can tell you about each Lego set. One of the wonderful things about working with kindergartners is the delight they take in their own knowledge. This unit channels that energy into writing. Kindergartners love being asked to teach you what they know and then to teach everyone and the world. This means, of course, that we need to let children in on the fact their beloved bicycle, their action figure collection, and their favorite topics—horses, dinosaurs—are book-worthy! During this unit of study, each child will write lots of information books about lots of different topics. As they do this, the work children will do aligns to the Common Core State Standards for kindergarten, which call for children to "use a combination of drawing, dictating, and writing to compose informative/explanatory texts in which they name what they are writing about and supply some information about the topic (W.K.2).

This is bound to be a time of excitement as children reveal and explore their hobbies and passions, from playing soccer to raising a parakeet. You can help children develop new, stronger nonfiction writing muscles by channeling them to choose topics about which they have knowledge. There are topics your kindergartners know better than *you* do, more than their peers. Your young writers need to recognize that their own lives are full of so much that they can teach others. This is an excellent opportunity to tap into children's funds of knowledge, to empower them to speak with authority and ownership about an aspect of their own life that is unique. One student may decide to write all about a sister who has Down's syndrome, another may write all about life in a new country, and another might write a guide to his or her neighborhood. The good news is that when any

Music in Our Hearts
Writing Songs and Poetry

RATIONALE/INTRODUCTION

Young children are natural poets. How many times have you watched a child tap her knees and chant lines of words to the beat? How many times have you seen a youngster spot a rabbit in the cloud or see swirls in the cement on the sidewalk? Young poets find significance in the ordinary details of their lives, draft with the intention of capturing life on the page, and learn from mentor authors. A unit of study on poetry, can teach children to write not only in that one particular genre but, also, to write better in general.

Across the unit, you will teach children to experiment with powerful language, to use line breaks, metaphor, and comparison to convey feelings. By the end of this study, your young writers will enjoy using both precise and also extravagant language to capture what they see and feel.

A SUMMARY OF THE BENDS IN THE ROAD FOR THIS UNIT

In Bend I (Immersion in Songwriting and Poetry: Setting the Stage), students will experience songs and poetry through their work in centers and through shared and interactive writing activities. It is during this week that students will get to experience many types of songs and poems.

In Bend II (Studying the Rhythm and Voice of Songs to Help Us Write Our Own), students will draw on Bend I in order to write their own songs. Students will begin to use tunes from familiar songs to jump-start their writing. They'll write lots of songs. Plan to spend another week working in this bend.

ALTERNATE UNIT
Music in Our Hearts:
Writing Songs and Poetry

IF you want to teach your students to become more conscious of the crafting and language decisions that writers make, THEN you might want to teach this unit.

> *"Despite the uniqueness of each child, there are particular ways they struggle, and predictable ways you can help. We can use all we know about child development, learning progressions, writing craft, and grade-specific standards to anticipate and plan for the individualized instruction our students are apt to need."*

Information Writing

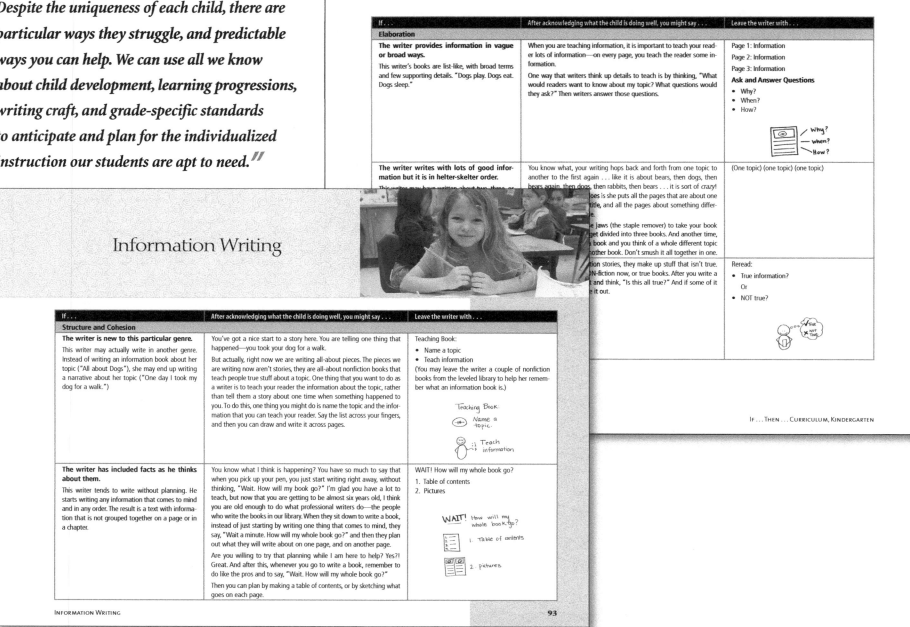

If...	After acknowledging what the child is doing well, you might say . . .	Leave the writer with . . .
Elaboration		
The writer provides information in vague or broad ways. This writer's books are list-like, with broad terms and few supporting details. "Dogs play. Dogs eat. Dogs sleep."	When you are teaching information, it is important to teach your reader lots of information—on every page, you teach the reader some information. One way that writers think up details to teach is by thinking, "What would readers want to know about my topic? What questions would they ask?" Then writers answer those questions.	Page 1: Information Page 2: Information Page 3: Information **Ask and Answer Questions** • Why? • When? • How?
The writer writes with lots of good information but it is in helter-skelter order. This writer may have written about two, three, or ... oes is she puts all the pages that are about one ... title, and all the pages about something differ... ...e jaws (the staple remover) to take your book ...get divided into three books. And another time, ... book and you think of a whole different topic ...other book. Don't smush it all together in one.	You know what, your writing hops back and forth from one topic to another to the first again . . . like it is about bears, then dogs, then bears again, then dogs, then rabbits, then bears . . . it is sort of *crazy*! ...tion stories, they make up stuff that isn't true. ON-fiction now, or true books. After you write a ...t and think, "Is this all true?" And if some of it ...e it out.	(One topic) (one topic) (one topic) Reread: • True information? Or • NOT true?

If . . .	After acknowledging what the child is doing well, you might say . . .	Leave the writer with . . .
Structure and Cohesion		
The writer is new to this particular genre. This writer may actually write in another genre. Instead of writing an information book about her topic ("All about Dogs"), she may end up writing a narrative about her topic ("One day I took my dog for a walk.")	You've got a nice start to a story here. You are telling one thing that happened—you took your dog for a walk. But actually, right now we are writing all-about pieces. The pieces we are writing now aren't stories, they are all-about nonfiction books that teach people true stuff about a topic. One thing that you want to do as a writer is to teach your reader the information about the topic, rather than tell them a story about one time when something happened to you. To do this, one thing you might do is name the topic and the information that you can teach your reader. Say the list across your fingers, and then you can draw and write it across pages.	Teaching Book: • Name a topic • Teach information (You may leave the writer a couple of nonfiction books from the leveled library to help her remember what an information book is.)
The writer has included facts as he thinks about them. This writer tends to write without planning. He starts writing any information that comes to mind and in any order. The result is a text with information that is not grouped together on a page or in a chapter.	You know what I think is happening? You have so much to say that when you pick up your pen, you just start writing right away, without thinking, "Wait. How will my book go?" I'm glad you have a lot to teach, but now that you are getting to be almost six years old, I think you are old enough to do what professional writers do—the people who write the books in our library. When they sit down to write a book, instead of just starting by writing one thing that comes to mind, they say, "Wait a minute. How will my whole book go?" and then they plan out what they will write about on one page, and on another page. Are you willing to try that planning while I am here to help? Yes?! Great. And after this, whenever you go to write a book, remember to do like the pros and to say, "Wait. How will my whole book go?" Then you can plan by making a table of contents, or by sketching what goes on each page.	WAIT! How will my whole book go? 1. Table of contents 2. Pictures

78

UNITS OF STUDY IN OPINION, INFORMATION, AND NARRATIVE WRITING • *If... Then... Curriculum: Assessment-Based Instruction, Kindergarten*

These charts will help you to anticipate, spot, and teach into the challenges your writers face during the independent work portion of your writing workshop. They lay out the specific strategy you might teach and the way you might contextualize the work for your writers.

If . . .	After acknowledging what the child is doing well, you might say . . .	Leave the writer with . . .
Language		
The writer does not use all that she knows about letter sounds/vowel patterns to write words. When you read the writer's work you see that she has one or two letter sounds in her labels. You know from your letter name/sound ID assessment that she knows the other letters and sounds that she is not putting onto the page. When you read the writer's work you see that she has a few words misspelled with vowel work that she is working on in word study. From your spelling assessment, for example, you know the writer knows or is working on short vowel patterns. In her work, though, she does not write with short vowel patterns.	When you write, you want to use all that you know about writing words. Using *all* that you know will help you as well as your reader to read back what you have written and taught in your book. One way that you can help make your writing even more readable is to work on getting more sounds in your words. After you put a letter down for your word, keep saying the word slowly. Listen for the next sound. Slide your finger under the letter you wrote as you listen to the next sound. Keep your alphabet chart here to think about what other letters you hear.	You may decide to have your student use her word sorts to help her study her spelling. Remind the writer to take out her sorts to remind her about the features of phonics that she is studying and working on. These could be in an envelope that she keeps in her writing folder if you make her a set.
The writer does not use domain-specific vocabulary. This writer has not included specialized words that fit with his topic. For example, if he is writing about dogs, he might say, "This is a dog. You need to walk your dog. Dogs need food. Dogs have babies." The writer does not specify what kind of a dog (a Spaniel or a Maltese), the type of food that dogs eat, or what you call baby dogs—puppies.	When you are teaching information in your books, remember that the reader *also* wants to be an expert. Usually experts know really important words that have to do with their topics. As a nonfiction writer you want to use these words and also teach them to your readers, so that they too can be experts. As you are writing, one way that you can do this [...] about the information and ask yourself, "Did I us[...] that fit with this information? Is there a better w[...] word that fits with this topic that I can use?"	A Post-it with a few keywords to reread and think about. You may write on the Post-it, "Look for places to use special words. Think about what important words fit with this topic."
The Process of Generating Ideas		
The writer chooses ideas that she likes rather than what she actually knows information about. This writer tends to pick topics that she does not know a lot of information about. Sometimes she picks topics according to things she likes or once saw on a television program. The writer does not pick topics with which she has had personal experience.	Sometimes it seems like you are trying to wri[...] about topics that you don't know too much abo[...] Writers write books about things that they know[...] so that they can teach others. They usually ch[...] have *a lot* to say about and that they think is i[...] know. There are many ways to come up with a topic t[...] think about your own life. What are things you h[...] things you do that you think other people shoul[...] Let's make a little list. Then you can start thinking about the chapters[...] to see if you have a lot to say about the topic.	

INFORMATION WRITING

If . . .	After acknowledging what the child is doing well, you might say . . .	Leave the writer with . . .
The Process of Drafting		
The writer spends more time elaborating on his drawing than using the picture to help add and write more information. This writer often does not spend the workshop time in an efficient way to get as much information and words as possible down on the page. He spends most of the workshop time drawing details onto the page, rather than using his drawing to get more words on the page.	Writers draw and write with details to teach the reader. Sometimes you may spend more time on your drawing because you see a lot of details that you can add. Remember, while writers are drafting, they are trying to get as much information into their words as possible. Drawings can help the writer see more to say. I want to teach you that when you are drafting and revising your information books, use what you draw to help add more information to your words. If the details don't really help you add more information, wait until the end of the writing process when you will publish to color and illustrate.	Use your picture to write all that you see.
The Process of Revision		
The writer is unsure how to revise her writing and does not use the various tools in the classroom. When this writer gets to the last page in her book, she may stop and get another booklet to begin a new text. The writer does not go back and try to add to her piece. She may or may not be aware of the charts, checklists, and mentor texts that she could use to help her decide how to revise her text.	Information writers revise as well. They use the same types of tools as other writers to help them revise their piece. Sometimes, studying a mentor text can help you find and think about what you may want to add or change in your own writing. One thing that I want to teach you is that you can study books and think, "What did this author do that was powerful in his writing? Can I do the same thing with my topic?"	A mentor text to help remind her to study books to find ideas for her writing. On a Post-it, write, "What did this author do that I can do?"
The writer tends to revise by elaborating, rather than narrowing and finding the focus of the text or chapter. When this writer revises, he may always revise to add information to his piece. Rarely will he think to take out something that doesn't go or to improve the way he has said something.	You are really good at adding things as you revise. Sometimes you add details, and sometimes you add things that will help make it so your writing makes sense. That's great. Congratulations. Now—can I teach you the next step? The next step as a reviser is to reread your writing, knowing that sometimes what the writing needs is for you to add, and sometimes the writing needs you to subtract! Like, if the book is called My Hamster and you get to a part that goes on and on about your turtle . . . what would you need to do? You are right! Subtract. And what if you say "My hamster has a tiny tail" at the start of your book and then at the very end you say, "My hamster has a tiny tail." What if you repeated yourself by mistake? You are right! You'd subtract. Writers even do one more thing when they revise, they sometimes try to write the same thing with better words, or more excitement—revising not to add or subtract but to improve. If you ever do that, would you call me over?	**Writers revise by:** • + adding (details, answers to readers questions) • – subtracting (parts that don't belong, repetition . . .) • improving (making the words better, making writing interesting)

Resources for Teaching Writing CD-ROM

The *Resources for Teaching Writing CD-ROM* for Kindergarten provides unit-specific print resources to support your teaching throughout the year. You'll find a rich assortment of instructional tools including **learning progressions, checklists and rubrics, correlations to the CCSS, paper choices,** and **teaching charts**. Offering daily support, these resources will help you establish a structured learning environment that fosters independence and self-direction.

Resources *for*
Teaching Writing
LUCY CALKINS

CD-ROM
Windows/PC or Macintosh

*first*hand
HEINEMANN
DEDICATED TO TEACHERS™

www.heinemann.com

Step 1

Warredey
Letsdo

cool
am ya
ok

Make sure
you make
the teams

Step 3

Step

Student writing samples illustrate different ways different students have exemplified the standard and highlight essential features of each writing genre.

" The writing workshop needs to be simple and predictable enough that your youngsters can learn to carry on within it independently. The materials and teaching tools you provide students will help you establish such a predictable, structured learning environment. "

80   UNITS OF STUDY IN OPINION, INFORMATION, AND NARRATIVE WRITING • *Resources for Teaching Writing CD-ROM*

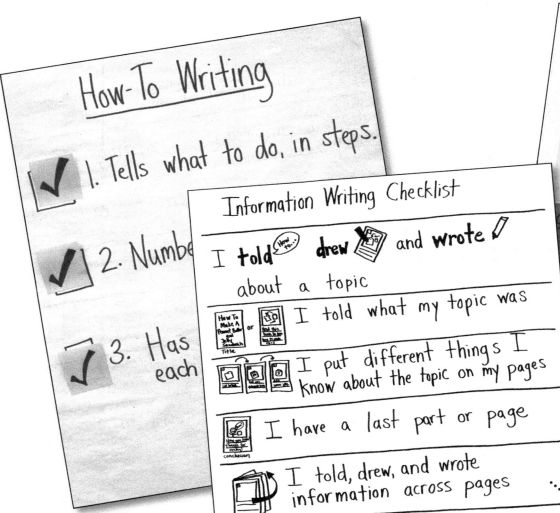

How-To Writing

☑ 1. Tells what to do, in steps.

☑ 2. Numbe[r]

☑ 3. Has
   each

Information Writing Checklist

I **told** (How To...) **drew** 🖼️ and **wrote** ✏️
about a topic

📄 or 📄 I told what my topic was
Title

🖼️🖼️🖼️ I put different things I
know about the topic on my pages

🖼️ I have a last part or page
conclusion

📚 I told, drew, and wrote
information across pages

★★★ I told, drew and wrote some
details about the topic

★ I told, drew and wrote some
important things about the topic

Writers Don't Say (How do you spell...?)

check the word wall
QQ ↓ Aa Bb Cc

use the room

s-t-r-e-t-ch

listen 😊 <

don't forget the vowel!
a e i o u

listen for little words
in to

A wide range of fresh-from-the-classroom instructional charts model proven teaching artifacts that are easy to copy and customize.

RESOURCES CD-ROM

Resources for Teaching Writing CD-ROM

Checklists of genre-specific writing criteria support self-assessment and goal setting, as well as writing rehearsal, revision, and editing.

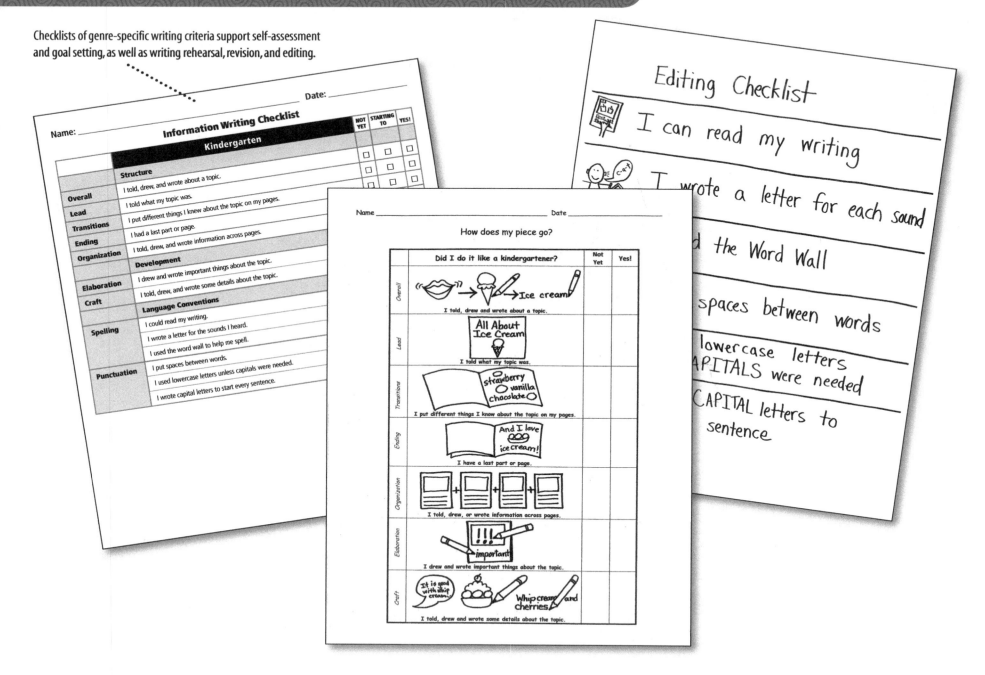

Common Core State Standards Alignment				
Session	**Writing Standards**	**Reading Standards**	**Speaking and Listening Standards**	**Language Standards**
1	W.K.2, W.K.5, **W.K.8**	RI.K.1, RI.K.6, RI.K.9, RI.1.6, RI.1.9	SL.K.1, SL.K.2, SL.K.3	L.K.1, L.K.2
2	**W.K.2**, W.K.5, W.1.2	RI.K.1	SL.K.1, SL.K.4, SL.K.5	L.K.1.e,f, L.K.2
3	**W.K.2**, W.K.5	RI.K.1, **RI.K.2**, RFS.K.1, RFS.K.2	**SL.K.1, SL.K.2, SL.K.3, SL.K.6**	L.K.1, L.K.2
4	**W.K.2**, W.K.5	RI.K.1	**SL.K.1.a, SL.K.2, SL.K.3, SL.K.6**	**L.K.1.d**, L.K.1, L.K.2
5	**W.K.2**, W.K.5	RI.K.7, **RFS.K.1.b**, RFS.K.3.a,b, RFS.1.3.a,b,d,e	SL.K.1, SL.K.5	L.K.1, L.K.2.c,d, L.K.6
6	**W.K.2**	RFS.K.3.c	SL.K.1	L.K.1., L.K.2
7	**W.K.2**, W.K.5, W.1.2	RI.K.1, RFS.K.1.b, RFS.K.3, RFS.1.3	SL.K.1, **SL.K.2, SL.K.3**	L.K.1, L.K.2.c,d, L.K.6
8	**W.K.2**, W.K.5, W.1.2	RI.K.1, **RI.K.7**, RI.1.1, RI.1.7	SL.K.1, SL.K.2, SL.K.3	L.K.1, L.K.2
9	W.K.2	RI.K.1	SL.K.1, SL.K.5	L.K.1, L.K.2, L.K.6, **L.1.1.j,d**
10	**W.K.3**, W.K.5, W.K.6, W.K.7, W.1.3	RI.K.1, **RFS.K.2, RFS.K.3**	SL.K.1, SL.K.2, SL.K.3, SL.K.6	**L.K.1**, L.K.2, **L.K.5.d**, L.K.6
11	**W.K.2**, W.K.5, W.1.2	RI.K.1, RI.K.2	SL.K.1, SL.K.2	L.K.1, L.K.2, L.K.6, **L.1.1.j**
12	**W.K.2**, W.K.5	RI.K.1	SL.K.1	L.K.1, L.K.2, L.K.5
13	W.K.2, **W.K.8**, W.1.7	RI.K.1	SL	
14	**W.K.2**	RI.K.1, RI.K.2	SL	
15	**W.K.2**, W.K.5, W.1.2	RI.K.1	SL	
16	W.K.2	RFS.K.1, RFS.K.3, RFS.1.3	SL	
17	**W.K.2**, W.K.5	RI.K.1	SL	
18	W.K.2, W.K.5, W.K.6	**RFS.K.1, RFS.K.3**	SL	
19	W.K.2, **W.K.5**	RFS.K.1, RFS.K.2, RFS.K.3	SL	

*Bold indicates major emphasis

Because writing workshop instruction involves students in writing, reading, speaking and listening, and language development, each session in each unit of study is correlated to the full Common Core State Standards for English Language Arts.

If/Then Conferring Scenarios help you assess student needs and differentiate instruction. Customizable conferring scenarios that can be printed on label paper provide students with artifacts from the day's lessons.

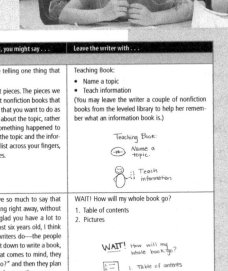

Information Writing

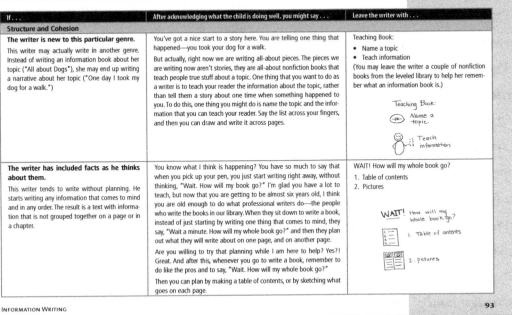

If . . .	After acknowledging what the child is doing well, you might say . . .	Leave the writer with . . .
Structure and Cohesion		
The writer is new to this particular genre. This writer may actually write in another genre. Instead of writing an information book about her topic ("All about Dogs"), she may end up writing a narrative about her topic ("One day I took my dog for a walk.")	You've got a nice start to a story here. You are telling one thing that happened—you took your dog for a walk. But actually, right now we are writing all-about pieces. The pieces we are writing now aren't stories, they are all-about nonfiction books that teach people true stuff about a topic. One thing that you want to do as a writer is to teach your reader the information about the topic, rather than tell them a story about one time when something happened to you. To do this, one thing you might do is name the topic and the information that you can teach your reader. Say the list across your fingers, and then you can draw and write it across pages.	Teaching Book: • Name a topic • Teach information (You may leave the writer a couple of nonfiction books from the leveled library to help her remember what an information book is.) *Teaching Book: Name a topic. Teach information*
The writer has included facts as he thinks about them. This writer tends to write without planning. He starts writing any information that comes to mind and in any order. The result is a text with information that is not grouped together on a page or in a chapter.	You know what I think is happening? You have so much to say that when you pick up your pen, you just start writing right away, without thinking, "Wait. How will my book go?" I'm glad you have a lot to teach, but now that you are getting to be almost six years old, I think you are old enough to do what professional writers do—the people who write the books in our library. When they sit down to write a book, instead of just starting by writing one thing that comes to mind, they say, "Wait a minute. How will my whole book go?" and then they plan out what they will write about on one page, and on another page. Are you willing to try that planning while I am here to help? Yes?! Great. And after this, whenever you go to write a book, remember to do like the pros and to say, "Wait. How will my book go?" Then you can plan by making a table of contents, or by sketching what goes on each page.	WAIT! How will my whole book go? 1. Table of contents 2. Pictures *WAIT! How will my whole book go? 1. Table of contents 2. pictures*

INFORMATION WRITING

93

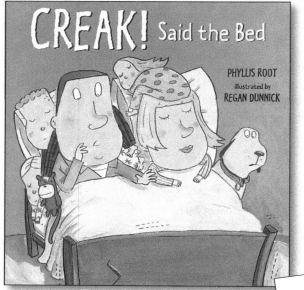

The **Kindergarten Trade Book Pack** includes three age-appropriate trade books that are used in the units to model effective writing techniques, encourage students to read as writers, and provide background knowledge.

▶ *Creak! Said the Bed* by Phyllis Root

▶ *Freight Train* by Donald Crews

▶ *My First Soccer Game* by Alyssa Satin Capucilli

Because some teachers may want to purchase class sets and others may already own these popular books, these are available as an optional, but recommended, purchase.

" Any effective writing curriculum acknowledges that it is important for writers to be immersed in powerful writing—literature and other kinds of texts. Children especially need opportunities to read as writers. By studying the work of other authors, students not only develop a felt sense of what it is they are trying to make but also learn the traditions of that particular kind of text. "